# GOD OF
# VENGEANCE

# GOD OF VENGEANCE

## DONALD MARGULIES

ADAPTED FROM THE PLAY BY
SHOLOM ASCH

BASED ON A LITERAL TRANSLATION BY
JOACHIM NEUGROSCHEL

THEATRE COMMUNICATIONS GROUP
NEW YORK
2004

*God of Vengeance* is published by Theatre Communications Group, Inc., 520 8th Avenue, 24th Floor, New York, NY 10018–4156.

This publication is made possible in part with public funds from the New York State Council on the Arts, a State Agency.

TCG books are exclusively distributed to the book trade by Consortium Book Sales and Distribution, 1045 Westgate Dr., St. Paul, MN 55114.

LIBRARY OF CONGRESS CATALOGING-IN-PUBLICATION DATA

Margulies, Donald.
God of vengeance / by Donald Margulies ; adapted from the play by Sholom Asch ; based on a literal translation by Joachim Neugroschel.
p. cm.
ISBN 1-55936-233-2 (pbk. : alk. Paper)
1. Lower East Side (New York, N.Y.)—Drama. 2. Tenement houses—Drama. 3. Jewish families—Drama. 4. Immigrants—Drama. I. Asch, Sholem, 1880–1957. Goòt fun neòkomeh. II. Title.
PS3563.A653 G64 2004
812'.54—dc22                     2003015700

Cover and text design by Lisa Govan
Cover photograph by Richard Feldman; Marin Hinkle (as Manke) in the 2002 Williamstown Theatre Festival production of *God of Vengeance*
Author photograph by Susan Johann

First Edition, February 2004

# INTRODUCTION

## *By Alisa Solomon*

I t's a Saturday night in 1923 in New York City. Imagine: You are the child of Jewish immigrant parents from Eastern Europe and you have recently moved away from the teeming poverty of the Lower East Side, where you grew up, into one of the newly prospering Jewish neighborhoods in the outer boroughs. As one of the many markers of your upward mobility—and as one of the means of cementing it—you are going to see a performance tonight. What you choose and how you engage it helps build your sense of yourself as an acculturated American.

It's a complicated and fascinating process—one that Donald Margulies critically evokes in his vivid adaptation of Sholom Asch's *God of Vengeance*, a play that itself stood at the center of debates over Jewish-American self-definition in 1923. Shifting the action from its original setting of 1906 Poland to the Lower East Side of New York in the early '20s, Margulies transports Asch's questions about piety and hypocrisy, love and transgression into the context of Jewish-American immigrant culture, where such issues were taking on new valences and urgency, especially for the second generation. For them, theatre was a site for working through experiences of Jewish dislocation and American acculturation, and for testing the boundaries of both Jewish and American normative identities. Margulies's version of *God of Vengeance* plays dynamically on the tensions reflected in and produced by this practice—the very tensions addressed thematically by the play, and also evoked by its public reception when presented on Broadway in 1923. By setting the play in this year, Margulies brings crucial context into the foreground; to fully appreciate his achievement, then, it's important to begin with that context.

This is the era of the Palmer Raids, an increasingly isolationist government, and tightened immigration laws, which deliberately choke off the influx of Jews from Eastern Europe. The Ku Klux Klan is flourishing, and the *Dearborn Independent*, Henry Ford's scurrilous newspaper, is circulated by the hundreds of thousands. "The American Jew does not assimilate," one typical article warns. "A Jewish American is a mere amateur gentile, doomed to be a parasite forever."

New York's stages, however, are telling a different story. On our Saturday night out in 1923, it isn't hard for newly middle-class Jewish New Yorkers—who probably make up at least a third of the audience—to find plays that acknowledge, in reaffirming and comforting ways, their increasing acceptance by mainstream America.

In the 1922–23 season alone, they can see on Broadway Anne Nichols's *Abie's Irish Rose*, the famed tearjerker about a marriage between a Jewish boy and an Irish girl, which, having opened in May 1922, remains one of the most popular plays of the season. (It will end up running for five years and

2,327 consecutive performances.) There's also Howard Rose's *Rosa Machree*, which tells the story of a young woman, daughter of a Jewish mother and an Irish father, set on winning over her stuffy and intolerant paternal grandfather. (The role was played to great acclaim by Julia Adler, daughter of the eminent Yiddish actor Jacob Adler.)

The same season also features John Galsworthy's *Loyalties*, in which Ferdinand de Levis, a newly assimilated and successful Jew, finds how hard it is actually to be accepted by the long-standing British upper-class when he justifiably accuses one of their number of stealing from him.

Whether the romantic youngfolk of *Rosa Machree* and *Abie's Irish Rose* or the decorous and genteel Ferdinand de Levis, Jewish protagonists on the Broadway stage of the early 1920s represent Jews in ways that make them feel good about who they are and want to be. While Abie's father is a comic stereotype right out of vaudeville—laughable Yiddish accent and all—Abie, just like the second-generation Jewish audience that adores him, can differentiate himself from the immigrant generation, remaining emotionally connected to his parents and their world even as he moves literally and figuratively away from it. Characters like Abie and Rose bear no traces of the old stage Jew's sing-song accent, wild gesticulations, grotesque appearance and devious dealings; they look, rather, like appealing, clean-cut American ingenues. They are recognizable as Jewish only because the text so names them, not because they bear any vestigial vaudevillian visual clues.

These new Jews, too, are nothing like the temptresses and lurkers in various Orientalist dramas of the season, such as *Desert Sands*—which the *New York Times* reviewer describes as presenting "the romance of the Sahara desert, the clash of

Oriental-Occidental natures, the rejuvenation in the hot east of a love between an Englishman and an Englishwoman that had been defeated in cold England." Likewise *The Voice from the Minaret*, about the liaison of two English runaways in Damascus, and *The Hindu*, about an English girl trapped in a lonely outpost, surrounded by treacherous, lecherous natives.

The exotic pulse of such works throbs, too, in the abundant Negro variety shows, such as *Dixie to Broadway*, featuring Florence Mills in banana headdress and grass skirt singing "Jungle Nights in Dixie Land" with a backup ensemble called the Plantation Chocolate Drops. Meanwhile, even gaudier and bawdier drag balls can be enjoyed by those willing to venture to Harlem, or to join the flock of conventional audiences at gay speakeasies that feature extravagant spectacles of open homosexuals singing and swishing around the stage.

At such shows, newly middle-class Jews can define themselves *against* these displays of racial and sexual difference, and place themselves within the category of normative Americans albeit with their own cherished—but less marked and less alien—ethnic identity.

While Abie and Rose are refined and controlled, the figures in the Negro revues, "pansy" shows and those lost-in-the-Orient plays, are made most threatening and foreign by virtue of one trait: They are sexually excessive. That's a charge that had long been flung at Jews as well (and would soon murderously reemerge in Europe). Indeed, pariah groups are often painted as slaves to their unquenchable lusts. Classic anti-Semitism typically described Jews as rampant sexual predators. Even the well-intentioned social reformers trying to provide uplift to the masses in the early years of the twentieth century decried the Lower East Side most of all for the sexual incontinence of its unwashed inhabitants. But the proudly *oys-gegrint* ("ungreened" or "no-longer-greenhorn") 1920s generation, which has moved en masse to the Grand Concourse and Brooklyn, is forging a respectable and restrained Jewish-American identity. The theatre is helping them do so.

Unless, that is, they choose among tonight's Broadway offerings Sholom Asch's *God of Vengeance*. Written in 1906 by one of the most prolific, popular and prickling authors of the explosive modern Yiddish literature movement, *Got fun Nekome* (as it's known in the original) is one of the toughest and most self-critical plays in the Yiddish canon. A moral melodrama, it focuses on Yankl Tshaptshovitsh, a man who runs a brothel, but has tried to raise his daughter Rivkele as a pure maiden, fit to be married off to a pious scholar. To win respectability— and a proper bridegroom for her—Yankl has undertaken the crowning communal good deed of commissioning a scribe to copy out a Torah, the sacred scroll containing the Five Books of Moses. Rivkele, however, has fallen in love with one of the women in her father's employ, and the play features steamy love scenes between them—as well as scenes of rabbinic hypocrisy and domestic violence. Exploring the moral predicaments of the clash between modern and traditional worlds in intimate, tragic terms, *Got fun Nekome* was enthusiastically received by popular audiences, and remained in the Yiddish repertoire for years. It sparked a spate of melodramatic prostitution plays—and even a Yiddish version of Shaw's *Mrs. Warren's Profession*. The English-language version, which opened on Broadway in 1923, was meant to be the crossover vehicle for the actor Rudolf Schildkraut, who hoped to follow his nephew, Joseph, to stardom on the all-American stage.

But Yankl Tshaptshovitsh looks more like one of those perfidious, lascivious rogues of the queer, Orientalist and Negro entertainments than like the noble Ferdinand de Levis or the lovestruck Jewish boy in *Abie's Irish Rose* (whose "queer" interethnic sexuality is contained by the resolution that blesses his marriage). Here's how one reviewer describes Schildkraut's performance: "He slaps his cheeks . . . pulls his hair and froth issues from his lips. He gurgles and mumbles, his eyes grow wet and glassy and he dies a dozen deaths."

Connecting this image of Yankl to the more general scene of criminality, prostitution and homosexuality, the daily reviewers reattached Jewish difference to depravity and foreignness. They attacked the production as un-American in its sexual excess. *God of Vengeance*, wrote Burns Mantle in the *Daily News*, is "an ugly story and hopelessly foreign to our Anglo-Saxon taste and understanding." The *Mail* concurred: "The play was a somber affair on one of those sordid themes which do not appeal to American tastes." The *Globe* reviewer said: "This is alien stuff, and, because alien, offensive." "It has," added the *Call*, "an unmistakable Oriental quality in its religious and ethical mood, in its sexual standards, and in the lyric beauty that gleams now and again out of the muck and filth of debased human life."

As is now well known, fifteen days after opening, the cast and the producer of *God of Vengeance* were arrested, and some months later, in an unprecedented ruling, a jury convicted them of promulgating obscenity.

What's striking is that the idea of obscenity argued in the press and in the court was not merely a matter of prostitutes—who were abundantly presented in a range of plays—or even lesbians who were presented unperturbed in the pansy shows. Rather, barely suppressed attitudes about the foreignness and sexual perversion of Jews were embedded within the more obvious charges of obscenity.

Thus, in the most central of cultural sites—the Broadway stage—the play hurls Jewish representation off the trajectory that has paralleled Jewish integration into the American mainstream (and that was supposed to do the same for Schildkraut's career). Instead of presenting Jews as recognizable and sympathetic to gentiles as well as to aspiring middle-class Jews, the English-language production of *God of Vengeance* displays Jews who are corrupt, sexually perverse, and altogether repellant. Here, they seem as foreign as the Negroes of the exploitative revues, as licentiously beyond the pale as the men in frills, tough dames and flaunting homosexuals of the pansy shows, as deceitful and dangerous as the Orientalist villains of colonialist dramas.

On their night on the town in 1923, Jews laboring to become white do not want to see flaunted on the Great White Way, a frothing, pimping, money-grubbing Yankl centerstage among a bunch of hookers, crooks and lusty lesbians. From an *oysgegrint* perspective, such images are not good for the Jews.

Though the second-generation Eastern European immigrants had not yet coalesced their numbers into political clout in the City, they could join the protests led by the more confident—and more assimilated—German Jews, who had been in the U.S. decades longer. Indeed, it was a German-Jewish Reform rabbi, Joseph Silverman, who first brought a complaint against the Broadway production, charging that it was anti-Semitic. "The play libels the Jewish religion," Silverman told Abe Cahan in an interview in the Yiddish newspaper *Forverts*. Debate churned in the Yiddish press more generally—and not without irony. After all, the Americanizing Jews who objected to exposing the Jewish underworld to the mainstream, were trying to distance themselves from the very community that read the Yiddish papers.

Nowadays, as new interest has been sparked in *God of Vengeance* after three-quarters of a century of almost complete neglect, these anxieties and tensions have been largely overlooked. Contemporary scholars, producers and theatre artists eager to recuperate the play within a narrative of gay and lesbian visibility on the American stage have concentrated, instead, on the sexual intrigue of the lesbian love story at its center and the scandal it provoked.

In the worst instances of the recent spate of *God of Vengeance* revivals—two Off-Off-Broadway productions I saw, for example—the play is approached with a shallow, prurient curiosity. These stagings focus on Rivkele and her paramour Manke, racing through the rest of the action like, well, two young lovers who can't wait to slip away from everyone and get their hands all over each other. It's the right energy for these characters, perhaps, but as an overall approach to the play it misses central themes, imagery and developments, treating them merely as exposition that needs to be endured as we await the juicy parts. In these productions, the company is at a loss for how to deal with the intricate, challenging ways in which the play considers and critiques its Jewish world.

This is one reason Donald Margulies's adaptation is so welcome and, in its own right, so important. In his version, the sexual conundrum is part of a tightly wound schema involving piety and peddling, familial demands and liberating desire, communal claims and the tug of social advancement, the shocking parallels between whoring and Torah. As for Asch, for Margulies, Rivkele and Manke's romance is not shocking, but matter-of-fact and endearing—indeed, theirs is the only relationship in the play that is tender and loving. What's more, the play displays both the brutality of men and the communal constraints on women—whose options, essentially, are to be sold as whores or as brides—and evokes an astonishing sympathy for their search for affection and self-sovereignty.

Little surprise that Margulies would be drawn to this work. Many of his own mordant plays—among them, *What's Wrong with This Picture?*, *The Loman Family Picnic* and *The Model Apartment*—probe what have become the comfortable tropes of comfortable Jewish life in late twentieth century America, skewing traditional takes on the Holocaust, the comedic (and theatrically commodified) Jewish family and assimilation. These works have twisted traditional dramatic structures into revealing distortions—parodying the Neil Simon comedy, inverting Arthur Miller, exploding the domesticating Holocaust drama.

Meanwhile, the Yiddish canon has been newly opened to Ashkenazi Jewish playwrights of Margulies's generation, who have begun taking a look at plays that work against the goopy sentimental image of the shtetl that has dominated so much mainstream nostalgia for the vanished world of their fathers. For one thing, this generation began wondering, too, about the world of the mothers. As a generation further removed from the Holocaust, they can take a clearer view of the shtetl and of the panoply of Jewish life of Eastern Europe: It's okay in the twenty-first century to acknowledge that Yiddish was not only the language of yeshiva *bokhers*, hand-wringing mamas, and affable dairymen, but also of pimps, prostitutes, hustlers and thieves. (That the Yiddish underworld would provide new fascination is also a result of the lack of availability of the shtetl to post-modern redefinition as contemporary Chasidim have come to monopolize the shtetl as mythic past.)

In his take on Asch's less misty mythic past, Margulies draws its conflicts closer to home: Yankl's brothel is depicted as a function of his drive to make a bundle and assimilate. Having changed his name to Jack Chapman—part of what he atones for as he descends into catastrophic collapse—he yearns to be precisely one of those Jewish up-and-comers who wants more than anything to be offended to see his story on Broadway in 1923. Today's audience must wonder: Is assimilation always a kind of pimping?

The first time I saw his version—at ACT Theatre in Seattle, directed by Gordon Edelstein—Margulies's antinostalgic depiction of the Lower East Side produced almost a Brechtian-like estrangement effect. It was so startling that a purely naturalistic response to the characters was impossible. What's more, the set he insists on, like Jo Mielziner's famous scenic design for *Death of a Salesman*, places a two-story structure right on stage, instead of changing the scene as the action moves from the upstairs home to the downstairs brothel. The coexistence of the two worlds dramatizes, through simultaneity, the parallels that Asch tends crudely to announce, allowing Margulies to show, for example, the johns handing over cash in the shadows below as Jack bargains away his daughter in the apartment above. Margulies thus streamlines and smooths over Asch's clunky dramaturgy, and condenses three sprawling acts to two that are tightly wound. These structural innovations help keep the tensions taut and the thematic contradictions on a high boil.

For instance, in the first scene, Rivkele and her mother Sara, chat upstairs about her upcoming wedding and await Rivkele's father, whom they describe as devout, dutiful and a bit of a disciplinarian. Meanwhile, in the dark beneath them, prostitutes greet and part from their johns. Soon a man in a dapper suit crosses the stage, enters the brothel and doles out cash to the girls. Then he goes upstairs: "Here's your father," Sara says. The audience audibly gasped, realizing for the first time that the pimp is the very man the women had been describing.

Stoking our astonishment throughout, Margulies keeps Asch's old antinomies kicking. Teasing out the pesky questions of spirit, love, family and commerce at the heart of Asch's play, Margulies, some eighty years after Schildkraut tried, has achieved crossover success, making *God of Vengeance* a profoundly compelling American play.

*New York City*
*January 2004*

# GOD OF
# VENGEANCE

.

Donald Margulies's version of *God of Vengeance* received its
world premiere at A Contemporary Theatre (Gordon Edelstein, Artistic Director; Jim Loder, Managing Director; Vito
Zingarelli, Producing Director) in Seattle, Washington, on
April 13, 2000. It was directed by Gordon Edelstein; the set
design was by Hugh Landwehr, the lighting design was by
Robert Wierzel; the original music and sound design were by
John Gromada, the costume design was by Anna Oliver, the
dramaturg was Liz Engelman, the dialect coach was Juli
Rosenzweig, the fight director was Geoffrey Alm and the
stage manager was Anne Kearson. The cast was as follows:

| | |
|---|---|
| JACK CHAPMAN | Matthew Boston |
| SARA | Nike Doukas |
| RIVKELE | Rachel Miner |
| MANKE | Naama Potok |
| HINDL | Johanna Melamed |
| SHLOYME | Mikael Salazar |
| REYZL | Betsy Schwartz |
| BASHA | Tricia Rodley |
| REB ELI | Larry Block |
| THE SCRIBE (REB AARON) | Sol Frieder |
| AN ORTHODOX MAN | Andrew Traister |

| | |
|---|---|
| LOWER EAST SIDE KIDS | Ian Nelson-Roehl, Scott Ross |
| THE PROSPECTIVE IN-LAW | Wauchor Stephens |
| INDIGENTS | Frank Krasnowsky, Jay A. Hurwitz |
| POOR WOMEN | Ilene Fins, Hinda Kipnis |
| PARTYGOERS, MINYAN | Mike Christensen, Matt Purvis, Joe Shapiro, Mary Unruh |

*God of Vengeance* was subsequently produced by the Williamstown Theatre Festival (Michael Ritchie, Producer; Jenny C. Gersten, Associate Producer; Deborah Fehr, General Manager) in Williamstown, Massachusetts, on July 21, 2002. It was directed by Gordon Edelstein; the set design was by Neil Patel, the lighting design was by Rui Rita, the original music and sound design were by John Gromada, the costume design was by Candice Donnelly, the production manager was Christopher Akins and the stage manager was Kelley Kirkpatrick. The cast was as follows:

| | |
|---|---|
| JACK CHAPMAN | Ron Liebman |
| SARA | Diane Venora |
| RIVKELE | Laura Breckenridge |
| MANKE | Marin Hinkle |
| HINDL | Jenny Bacon |
| SHLOYME | Bruce MacVittie |
| REYZL | Jenn Lee Harris |
| BASHA | Christy Meyer |
| REB ELI | Larry Block |
| THE SCRIBE (REB AARON) | Sol Frieder |
| AN ORTHODOX MAN | Joel Rooks |

| | |
|---|---|
| IRISH KID | Michael Jerrod Moore |
| SECOND KID | Aaron Paternoster |
| THE PROSPECTIVE IN-LAW | Mort Broch |
| FIRST INDIGENT | Daniel Deferrari |
| SECOND INDIGENT | Lee Rosen |
| FIRST POOR WOMAN | Rosalind Cramer |
| SECOND POOR WOMAN | Joyce Lazarus |
| POOR PEOPLE/<br>PARTYGOERS | Sarah Bellows, Nancy Burnstein, Natalie Jacobson, Melissa Miller, Noam Rubin, Eric Neher |
| POOR PEOPLE/MINYAN | Cy Beer, Robert James, Michael Lively, Constantine Maroulis, Eric Neher, Ben Russo, Benjamin Strands, Mark Weimer |

The author is grateful to all of the aforementioned people for bringing this behemoth to life, particularly Michael Ritchie and the irrepressible Gordon Edelstein.

## Characters

JACK CHAPMAN

SARA

RIVKELE

MANKE

HINDL

SHLOYME

REYZL

BASHA

REB ELI

THE SCRIBE (REB AARON)

AN ORTHODOX MAN

IRISH KID

SECOND KID

THE PROSPECTIVE IN-LAW

FIRST INDIGENT

SECOND INDIGENT

FIRST POOR WOMAN

SECOND POOR WOMAN

POOR PEOPLE/MINYAN

PARTYGOERS

PLACE

The Lower East Side of New York

TIME

1923

# ACT ONE

The Lower East Side of New York. 1923.

    *The set consists of a two-story cross-section of a tenement build-ing, the suggestion of an alleyway, a sidewalk and a stoop. The tall buildings of the city loom in the background.*

    *The upstairs apartment is living quarters to Jack Chapman, a.k.a. Yankel Tshaptshovitsh, his wife Sara, and their daughter Rivkele. The kitchen and master bedroom are not visible but the living/dining room and Rivkele's girlish bedroom are. The living room, decorated with framed family photos and a variety of* tschatchkes, *is an incongruous mix of old world quaintness and greenhorn pretension. A fire escape is the urban balcony outside Rivkele's window, with a ladder that leads to the alley.*

    *Downstairs, below the staid residence, is a brothel. Brass beds are partly concealed in cubicles behind exotic curtains. A chaise splashed with colorful fabrics is prominently placed in the main reception area. Washstand, liquor stash, Victrola, lamps, secondhand chairs. The walls are decorated with mismatched ornate mirrors and various pictures of women in seductive poses.*

*A collage of sounds of the teeming city. Lights up: a spring after-noon. We find Rivkele, seventeen years old, sitting forlornly at her win-dow, like a Jazz-Age Rapunzel, humming a Yiddish song while embroidering a vestment.*

*Manke, a streetwalker in her twenties, walks on and fixes her lip-stick while looking in a compact. An Orthodox Man of late middle-age nervously shields his face as he walks past, but not without notic-ing Manke. Manke, standing near the stoop, lights a cigarette.*

*Sara comes on, her baskets full of challahs and flowers.*

SARA *(To Manke)*: Move.

*(Manke blows smoke in Sara's face and giggles.)*

Very funny.

*(Sara goes upstairs where she puts the flowers in a vase and put-ters around the living room, sets a buffet table, etc.*
*Rivkele sees Manke from her window. Her face brightens.)*

RIVKELE *(Calls in a whisper)*: Manke!

*(Manke's face loses its hardness when she sees Rivkele.)*

MANKE: Rivkele!
RIVKELE: I prayed you'd be there. I said, please, God, I'm going to look out my window, please let Manke be there. And you were!
MANKE: Shh shh shh.
RIVKELE: Look at my stitching. See? I'm doing as you said. *(Shows her the vestment)*

MANKE: Yes! You're such a good pupil.

RIVKELE: I want to see you so much.

MANKE: Me, too. Come down!

RIVKELE: I can't. My father's having a party. And I'm the guest of honor.

(*The Orthodox Man returns and nervously makes his move; he clears his throat to get Manke's attention.*)

ORTHODOX MAN: Can we go somewhere?

MANKE: Yeah, sure. Right this way.

(*She takes a final puff and grinds out the cigarette, then blows a kiss to Rivkele and whispers:*)

Later.

(*Rivkele waves ruefully. She works on a paper flower chain as Manke leads the man into the downstairs apartment. He warily follows, kissing the* mezuzah *on his way in.*)

ORTHODOX MAN: So this is what it looks like.

MANKE: You were expecting the Waldorf-Astoria?

ORTHODOX MAN: You hear about such a place your whole life . . . your imagination . . .

MANKE: It's just a place. Four walls, beds that sag in the middle. My bed is here.

(*She pulls open the drape on her cubicle and steps out of her dress.*)

ORTHODOX MAN: No no no. Not so fast. (*A beat*) Could we maybe talk a little first?

MANKE: Talk?

ORTHODOX MAN: Yeah. *You* know. Talk.

MANKE: We didn't come here for conversation.

ORTHODOX MAN: I know. But, please. Let's sit a minute.

*(He sits down on the chaise. She shrugs, then sits next to him. Silence.)*

MANKE: *Nu?* (*Meaning, Well . . . ?*)

ORTHODOX MAN: I walked down this street so many times. Summer, winter. Went out of my way. Just to see you.

MANKE: Oh, yeah? You'd gawk at me, then go home, screw your wife?

ORTHODOX MAN: No. (*A beat*) I just got up from *shiva.*

MANKE: Oh. I'm sorry.

ORTHODOX MAN (*Nods his thanks*): She was sick a long time, my wife, may she rest in peace. A long time.

*(Manke nods. Silence. He sighs deeply, inhales her aroma.)*

What is that?

MANKE: Rose water. I dab some on my neck.

*(She lifts her hair so he can smell her neck. He nearly swoons, gets up, moves away.)*

What.

ORTHODOX MAN: I never should've come.

MANKE: Why not?

ORTHODOX MAN: It's a sin! That's why not! What goes on here are sinful things!

*(She laughs.)*

What's so funny?

MANKE: Sin now, atone later. That's what they all do.

*(Her laughter subsides. He's charmed.)*

ORTHODOX MAN: What's your name?

MANKE: Manke.

ORTHODOX MAN: Manke?! Is that so? I knew a girl named Manke, once.

MANKE: Yeah, yeah, I've heard that one before.

ORTHODOX MAN: No, I did. In the old country. Back in Vilna.

MANKE: Vilna?! You're from Vilna?

ORTHODOX MAN: Yes.

MANKE: I'm from Vilkia.

ORTHODOX MAN: Vilkia! Small world! My mother was born in Vilkia. Her name was Zide.

MANKE *(Can't recall, shrugs)*: I left a long time ago. I was only seven.

ORTHODOX MAN: A child.

MANKE: Once.

ORTHODOX MAN: You're still a child.

MANKE: No. Not anymore. Not for a long time.

ORTHODOX MAN: Oh, but you are. Look at that *punim*. How does a girl with a face like an angel end up doing something like this?

MANKE *(Brusquely gets up)*: Look, I don't want to talk anymore. Okay? No more talking. Talking's never a good idea. I wanna dance.

ORTHODOX MAN: Dance?

*(She goes to the Victrola, puts on a jaunty Tin Pan Alley tune.)*

MANKE: There! Come on, let's dance!

*(She pulls him to his feet. He resists.)*

ORTHODOX MAN: No, no, I can't . . .
MANKE: What do you mean, you can't?
ORTHODOX MAN: It's not allowed . . .
MANKE: "Not allowed"?! Mister! You'll pay to *shtup* me but you won't dance with me?

*(She snatches his hat, puts it on her head and teasingly dances around him.)*

ORTHODOX MAN: Hey! What are you doing?! You mustn't do that! Give it back!

*(She gets him to move with her, awkwardly, in a dance-like way. He succumbs to her charms in spite of himself. Manke takes off the man's jacket, revealing his traditional garb underneath, and dons the jacket herself. She performs a seductive, sexually charged dance.*

*Meanwhile, upstairs, Rivkele hears the music and dances freely, almost erotically, around her room. Wrapped in her paper flower chain, her romantic reverie is shattered by her mother's call.)*

SARA *(Putting on an apron)*: Rivka!

*(Rivkele, breathless, stands guiltily in her doorway.)*

What are you doing in there? The whole house is shaking.

RIVKELE: Nothing.

SARA: Well, come. Finish with the decorations.

*(Sara continues bustling about. Rivkele drapes paper flowers around the room.*

*Downstairs, Manke's dance with the Orthodox Man has become more sultry. Trembling, he kisses her face. She turns off the music and, her back to him, walks to her cubicle and waits at the curtain. He braces himself and follows her in.)*

ORTHODOX MAN: *Oy gevalt. (As in, What am I doing?)*

*(As the Orthodox Man sits on the bed and begins to remove his shoes, Manke looks at her watch, then draws the drape.*

*Upstairs, Rivkele and Sara continue their preparations.)*

RIVKELE *(Decorating the mirror)*: Look, Mama. Look how pretty it looks.

SARA: Yes, yes, very pretty. Stop dreaming. We want to be finished by the time your father gets home. Here, set these out.

*(She gives Rivkele breads, etc., which the girl arranges.)*

RIVKELE: Will there be music at this party?

SARA: Music? What kind of music?

RIVKELE: I don't know, a little Sophie Tucker, maybe?

SARA: Sophie Tucker?! Your father wants to impress the men from the synagogue; all he would need is Sophie Tucker. He invited the whole neighborhood, practically, your

father. If everyone comes who was invited . . . I hate to
think what they'll do to this place. I should've rolled up
my rugs.

RIVKELE: Will girls be coming, too?

SARA: Girls? Maybe. Some people might bring their daughters. Nice Jewish girls.

RIVKELE: Will the girls from downstairs be coming?

SARA (*Stops puttering*): The girls from downstairs? What do
*you* think? (*Resumes puttering*)

(*During the above, Basha and Reyzl, two hookers both barely in
their twenties, enter with two East Side kids. One of the kids is
more confident than the other, who lags behind. They go into the
brothel.*)

IRISH KID (*Coaxing his reluctant friend*): Come on! Come on!

BASHA: You boys sure you want to go through with this?

IRISH KID: Sure we're sure.

BASHA: 'Cause you don't have to.

IRISH KID: We're sure, we're sure.

REYZL (*To Basha*): Look how cute, they could be our kid
brothers.

IRISH KID: Hey! We ain't your kid brothers.

REYZL (*Feigns being impressed*): Oh, well, pardon me!

IRISH KID: We been with plenty of girls.

BASHA: Okay, Casanova, who gets who?

IRISH KID: I'll take you.

BASHA: Yeah? That okay with your friend?

IRISH KID: He don't care.

BASHA: Oh. Okay. (*Starts to lead him inside*)

REYZL (*To Kid Two*): Well . . . ? You coming, or what?

KID TWO: Yeah. *(Takes a step, then backs away)* Uh, on second
 thought, there's something I gotta do . . . See ya, Francis . . .
 *(He runs down the street)*

BASHA *(Teasing)*: "Francis"?

REYZL *(Overlapping, as Kid Two goes)*: Hey! What's the matter,
 you don't like my looks?!

IRISH KID: Ah, don't mind him. He's chicken. Hey, why don't
 you come, too?

REYZL: What do you mean?

IRISH KID: *You* know. You, me, and her.

REYZL: That's a new one, huh, Basha?

BASHA *(To the Irish Kid)*: You like Jewish girls?

IRISH KID: I like girls.

REYZL: It's gonna cost you double.

IRISH KID: I don't care. *(Shows his cash. Grins)* Moron gave me
 his money.

*(Reyzl and Basha giggle as the threesome enter a cubicle and close
the drape.*
 *Upstairs:)*

RIVKELE: What about dancing, Mama? Will there be dancing?

SARA: I said I didn't know if there was gonna be *music.*

RIVKELE: Oh, I hope so. I hope there *is* dancing. There's never
 any music in this house. Or dancing. I love to dance. I wish
 I had a silk dress and elegant, ladylike shoes to dance in,
 not these clumsy old schoolgirl shoes.

SARA: You wear schoolgirl shoes, my dear, because you are a
 girl! I hate to break it to you!

RIVKELE: But I'm not! I'm seventeen! Papa makes me wear
 these silly little dresses.

SARA: Don't let your father hear you talk like that. He takes such pride in you!

RIVKELE: Pride?! Like for a puppy, yes. Or a doll. For him to dress up and do with as he pleases.

SARA: Let me tell you something, darling. Your father may be smart about a lot of things but about women . . . ? *(She shakes her head)* Let me give you a little advice: Take what you can get from him. That's what I do.

RIVKELE: If only I could have some new clothes. Like I see in *Harper's Magazine.*

SARA: Well, once you're married, young lady—God willing, come *Shevuas*—you'll be free to dress . . . however your *husband* sees fit.

RIVKELE: But I'm grown up already.

SARA: You're hardly grown up.

RIVKELE: Look at me, Mama.

SARA: Yeah, yeah, very nice.

RIVKELE: Stop what you're doing and look at me.

*(She makes Sara stop and actually look at her.)*

I am not a child. Am I.

SARA *(A realization)*: No. No, you're not.

RIVKELE *(Pinches her shirtwaist)*: See? I have breasts. And a waist. Manke says—

SARA: Manke!

RIVKELE: Manke says I have a very nice shape.

SARA: Oh, she does.

RIVKELE: She has all these beautiful clothes she says she'd let me wear.

SARA: Oh, really? I've got news for you: You're not putting on any of Manke's clothes.

RIVKELE: You should see, her closet is filled with—! (*She stops herself*)

SARA: Manke's closet? What do you know from Manke's closet?

RIVKELE (*A confession*): I've been down there.

SARA: Is that so?

RIVKELE: She's been teaching me how to embroider. Remember you said it would be good for me to learn?

SARA: I didn't mean for you to go down there!

RIVKELE: Then how, Mama, how was I to learn? She's taught me a lot. Wait, let me show you.

(*She goes to her room to get the embroidered vestment.*)

SARA (*Calls*): You know the rules. If your father ever found out!

RIVKELE (*Returns, holds up the vestment*): See? She's such a good teacher. See how well she draws? She drew the Star of David and the olive leaves. Just like the vestment in synagogue.

SARA (*Impressed*): Manke did this?

RIVKELE: Yes. Isn't it beautiful?

SARA: Whatever you do, don't tell your father Manke had anything to do with this. He'd have a fit.

RIVKELE: I thought it would please him.

SARA: Please him?! It *wouldn't* please him—that you were getting embroidery lessons downstairs from Manke?! That her dirty hands touched something as sacred as this?!

RIVKELE: Dirty hands? Oh, no, Manke's hands aren't dirty. She's my friend.

SARA: Your "friend." *Uy gut.* He doesn't want you mixing with the girls downstairs. That's all there is to it.

*(Downstairs, the Irish Kid, wearing only his underwear and holding his clothes in a bundle, comes out of the cubicle and hurriedly gets dressed. Basha, wrapped in a sheet, and Reyzl follow.)*

BASHA: That was fast.
REYZL: I never even got my turn.
BASHA: What's the matter, "Francis"? Got a train to catch?

*(The girls laugh derisively.)*

IRISH KID: Screw you.
BASHA: You wish.

*(He starts to go.)*

REYZL: Hey, where you going? Pay up!

*(Jack Chapman, a.k.a. Yankel Tshaptshovitsh, comes down the street with a bounce in his step.)*

BASHA: Hey! Mister! Stop him!
REYZL: He didn't pay! He owes us both!
JACK *(Stops the Irish Kid, roughs him up)*: Oh, is that so? Trying to get a free ride, huh? Huh?
IRISH KID *(Overlapping)*: Hey! Leave me alone! Let go of me!
JACK: Nobody gets a free ride. You understand? Nobody!
IRISH KID: Get offa me—kike!
JACK *(More incensed)*: Why you little *pisher*! Who do you think you are? Huh?! Pay up! You hear me? Hand it over! Before I wring your pimply little neck!
IRISH KID *(Overlapping)*: Here! Take it! Here's your stinking money!

*(He crumples the money and tosses it to the ground.)*

JACK: Good! Now get the hell outta here! Go!

*(He pushes the Irish Kid, who runs away. He shouts after him:)*

And don't show your little Irish putz around here again! *Shaygetz! (He picks up the bills and smoothes them out. To the girls)* What are *you* looking at?

*(They remain silent. He gives them each a dollar and puts the rest in his billfold. He changes his mind and gives them more.)*

All right, now go fix yourselves up. Go on.

*(Jack putters downstairs while Reyzl and Basha get dressed, fix their makeup.*
*Meanwhile, upstairs:)*

RIVKELE: Does Papa really think I don't know what goes on down there? When I was old enough to ask questions, you know what he told me? He said it was a boarding house down there! A boarding house!

*(Reyzl and Basha reemerge, Jack eggs them on; the girls go.)*

JACK: The night is young. Go go go!
SARA *(To Rivkele)*: Never mind, you! Everything that man has done—good or bad—he's done for you.
RIVKELE: I know, Mama.
SARA: He's trying so hard to change his ways. Give him a lit-tle credit, will you? *(Hears him coming up the stairs)* Shhh.

Here he comes. Please, darling? Be a good girl. Try to show your gratitude. It costs a lot to be pious.

(*Jack bursts ebulliently into the room.*)

JACK: Well! Let me tell *you*: Everybody is talking about this party! And I mean everybody!

SARA: Oh, yeah?

JACK: Sara, the whole neighborhood is talking. I saw Dr. Cohen on the street.

SARA: Dr. Cohen! Is that so!

JACK: Oh, yeah, I'm telling you: *Everybody*. He was quite grateful for the invitation, Dr. Cohen, wished us all the best.

SARA: Dr. Cohen is coming here?

JACK: Well, no, not exactly. He's a very important man that Dr. Cohen.

SARA: I know!

JACK: You should have seen: He was rushing to the hospital with his little black bag when I saw him. A woman was giving birth, he told me; he couldn't talk, he had to run. I don't envy *his* life, let me tell *you*. Klein, the tailor, I saw him, too.

SARA: And?

JACK: He said he would try.

SARA: Try?! That doesn't help me. I need to know who's coming. What if there's not enough food?

JACK: There's enough, there's enough! Relax! *I'm* the one who should be nervous. My name is on the line, that's all. Big deal, what's a name? Oh, I even invited a bunch of unfortunate souls off the streets, so the *machers* will see what a big-hearted *mensch* I am.

SARA: Jack!

JACK (*Gently corrects her*): Yankel, Yankel, remember? No more Jack, I'm Yankel again.

SARA: Forgive me: *Yankel*. It's still so new, I keep forgetting.

JACK (*To Rivkele, who has been trying to disappear*): What, you don't say hello to your father anymore? (*To Sara*) She doesn't say hello?

(*Sara nudges Rivkele.*)

RIVKELE: Hello, Papa.

JACK (*Teasing*): "Hello, Papa." Come here, I'm not gonna bite you. (*Sees the vestment*) What's that she's holding?

SARA (*To Rivkele*): Show him.

RIVKELE (*Displays it*): It's a vestment, Papa. For the Torah.

JACK: For the—? Well, how do you like that?! Isn't that wonderful? Where'd it come from?

SARA: Tell him. (*Rivkele says nothing; to Jack*) She made it.

JACK (*To Sara*): No! Yes?

SARA: Yes; she did.

JACK (*To Rivkele*): Bring it closer, let me see.

SARA (*Quietly prodding*): Go on.

(*Rivkele tentatively offers it to Jack. He takes it. He's effusive.*)

JACK: Will you look at this! Isn't that gorgeous?!

SARA: Yes; it is.

JACK: Such talent! Who knew my little Rivkele had not only beauty but talent? (*To Sara*) Did you?

SARA: Not me.

JACK: It looks professional. Doesn't it?

SARA (*Nods, while exchanging looks with Rivkele*): Yes; it does.

JACK (*To Rivkele*): You did this all by yourself?

SARA: With her own two hands.

JACK: Where'd she learn how to make a beautiful thing like this?!

SARA (*Shrugs*): Here and there.

JACK (*To Sara*): You see that? You think you know your own child and then she does something like this? Come, darling, let me give you a kiss.

(*Rivkele is reluctant.*)

What, you won't let your father kiss you?

SARA: Your father wants to kiss you. Go.

(*A beat. Rivkele tentatively goes to him. He pats his lap. Uncomfortably, Rivkele sits on his lap. He kisses her cheek.*)

JACK: Well, now! Was that so terrible? (*To Sara*) She's getting so grown up she doesn't like to sit on her papa's lap anymore?

SARA (*Shrugs, then*): I've got to check on that goose.

RIVKELE (*Suddenly*): No, Mama! (*She doesn't want to be left alone*)

SARA: What? It's *shpritzing* fat all over everything. (*To Jack*) You had to have goose . . .

(*Sara goes offstage to the kitchen. Jack bounces Rivkele on his knee while humming a Yiddish song. She gets up.*)

JACK: What's the matter? You used to love sitting on my lap.

RIVKELE: I'm too big to sit on your lap.

JACK: Don't be ridiculous. You're still my little girl. Remember we used to ride to Coney Island on Sundays in the summertime, just the two of us, you on my lap? Trolley after trolley, all the way to the end of the line, till we could smell the ocean? And I'd buy you salt water taffy and you'd laugh and chase the waves in your little bathing costume?

RIVKELE: That was a long time ago, Papa.

JACK: How long ago could it be? You're still a child. It seems like yesterday. (*A beat*) Something happened. What happened?

RIVKELE: Things changed.

JACK: What changed?

RIVKELE: I grew up.

JACK: No no. Why did we stop going? You lost interest in taffy and the long trolley ride, what?

RIVKELE: Papa, may I go to my room now?

JACK (*Incensed*): No! When I tell you to go to your room, then you may go!

(*She is silent; he is remorseful.*)

Rivkele . . . Come back. I don't mean to yell. You know how much your papa loves you, don't you?

RIVKELE (*With a sigh*): Yes, Papa.

JACK: To the ends of the earth, that's how far I would go.

RIVKELE: I know, Papa. I know.

JACK: All I want . . . I want you should marry well and have children. I want you should walk down the street with dignity! So when people see you—the so-called respectable people—they look you in the eye; not down at your feet. (*He takes her hand*) Sweetheart, God is being invited back into this house. You'll see. Things are gonna be different. I promise. *I'm* gonna be different. Once I get that Torah for you ... A holy man, a scribe, wrote one by hand, in beautiful script, for a man who died. He's coming here, this scribe; Reb Eli is bringing him. And I'm offering him a helluva lotta money for it, too, believe me. But, hey, I don't care about that; that's not important. What *is* important is *you. Your* welfare. *Your* future. *(Beaming)* Eli's been playing matchmaker. He's got his eye on someone for you. A scholar.

*(Uncomfortable, she moves away.)*

What's wrong?

*(She shakes her head, evades him. Sara returns from the kitchen.)*

SARA: Uch! Goose fat all over everything. I should make soap.
JACK *(To Sara)*: I'm embarrassing her. Marriage talk has made her bashful.
SARA: Marriage is God's will. What's to be bashful about? God knows everybody does it.
JACK *(To Rivkele)*: See? What would you like?
RIVKELE: What do you mean?
JACK: I want to buy you something, a little present. *(Takes out his billfold)* What should it be?

*(Rivkele doesn't answer.)*

Hm?

SARA *(To Rivkele)*: Cat got your tongue? Your father wants to buy you something. *(Sotto)* Take him up on his offer.

JACK: Let's see . . . should it be a doll? A little rag doll? Huh? What.

SARA: She'd like a silk dress and a pair of pretty shoes.

JACK: A silk dress and a pair of shoes? What's wrong with the dresses she has?

SARA: You asked what she wanted.

JACK *(To Rivkele)*: Is that what you'd like?

*(She nods.)*

Then why didn't you say so? Here, go buy yourself that dress and those shoes. *(He gives her money)* You don't know how to say thank you?

RIVKELE: Thank you, Papa. May I go to my room now?

JACK: Okay. Now you may go.

*(Rivkele exits to her room.)*

*(Calling)* You'll come out for the party, though, won't you.

RIVKELE: Yes, Papa.

*(She exits into her room.*
*A pause.)*

JACK: What's with her?

SARA *(Shrugs)*: It's the age.

JACK: What more can I do for her than I'm already doing?

SARA: Nothing.

JACK: Sometimes I think she doesn't like me.

SARA: Jack.

JACK (*Corrects her*): Yankel. It's true, Sara. I feel like she's passing judgment all the time.

SARA: It's the age.

JACK: I feel like everybody has an opinion about me, and it's not very good.

SARA: What, all of a sudden, in the middle of your life, it matters to you what people think?, what God thinks?

JACK: Of course it matters. What, it shouldn't?

SARA: Public opinion never stopped you before.

JACK: I was never in the middle of my life before. I'm gonna be dead one day, you know.

SARA: God forbid.

JACK: No, honestly. I ask myself, Do I give a damn what people will have to say about me when I'm dead? And the answer comes back, Yeah, I do, I do care. It's not too late to change.

SARA: Well, don't expect miracles. That's all I'm saying. God doesn't hand out miracles like the pickle man from his pushcart.

(*Feeling affectionate, he comes up behind her.*)

JACK: You're funny.

SARA: Ha ha.

JACK (*Calls her by her Yiddish diminutive*): Soyreleh.

SARA: Uy. "Soyreleh" now.

(*He nuzzles his face in her neck.*)

What are you doing?

JACK: Can't I have a nibble?

SARA: Nibble.

*(Pause. He kisses her neck while she gazes into space.)*

When I think of the life I would've had if I'd never met
you . . .

JACK *(A beat; his ardor cooled)*: You would have died on the
street. *(A beat)* I'm gonna change my clothes.

*(He exits. Sara finishes what she's doing, then goes off to the
kitchen.*

*During the above, Rivkele, in bed embroidering, hits a snag,
struggles with it, then decides to find Manke. The vestment in
hand, Rivkele climbs out of her window, down the fire escape, and
stealthily enters the brothel.)*

RIVKELE *(Whispers)*: Manke?

*(A moan draws her to Manke's cubicle, from which we hear
creaking bed springs. Rivkele's impulse is to go but she stops herself and stays to eavesdrop, becoming excited by what she hears.*

*Meanwhile, on the street: Shloyme, a flashily dressed, street-
wise felon, appears, a ribbon-wrapped bundle tucked under his
arm. Two hungry Indigents approach from the opposite direction.
They converge at the stoop.)*

SHLOYME *(Unfriendly)*: Can I help you?

FIRST INDIGENT: This Jack Chapman's place?

SHLOYME: Yeah, what can I do for you?

FIRST INDIGENT: He told us to come.

SHLOYME: Oh, yeah?

SECOND INDIGENT: We're a little on the early side.

SHLOYME: Early for what? You're never too early around here. There's always some girl.

SECOND INDIGENT: Girl?

SHLOYME: Yeah. You're here for the girls, right?

FIRST INDIGENT (*Realizing the misunderstanding*): Oh, no, not the girls, the goose.

SHLOYME: The goose?

FIRST INDIGENT: Yeah, he told us he's having a party.

SECOND INDIGENT: A party for his daughter.

SHLOYME: A party, huh? What kind of party?

SECOND INDIGENT: Don't ask me.

FIRST INDIGENT: All I know is he said something about a Torah scroll and a goose.

SHLOYME: A Torah scroll? We talking about the same Jack Chapman?

SECOND INDIGENT: Is this his place or not?

SHLOYME: Yeah, this is it. Be my guests, go right on up.

INDIGENTS: Thanks. So long.

SHLOYME (*Calling as they go*): And save me a piece of that bird!

(*The Indigents go upstairs. Both Sara and Jack are offstage. The Indigents admire the room and the spread and begin to put food in their pockets.*

*Meanwhile, Shloyme enters the downstairs apartment and is surprised and amused to see Rivkele listening at Manke's cubicle.*)

Well, well, well . . .

(*Rivkele gasps. He approaches.*)

If it ain't little Goldilocks. What you doing down here, Goldilocks? Picking up a few pointers? (*Mimics panting; cracks himself up*)

RIVKELE (*Embarrassed*): I'm sorry . . .

(*She tries to go past; he blocks her.*)

SHLOYME: Where you going? (*Admiringly*) Look at *you*! You filled out awfully nice . . .

RIVKELE: Please . . .

SHLOYME: Don't go on my account. Sit. Stay and chat a while.

(*He takes her hand, sits her down beside him on the sofa.*)

RIVKELE: Please, I have to go back up. I didn't mean to . . .

SHLOYME (*Takes out a Baby Ruth, unwraps it suggestively*): Want a bite?

(*She shakes her head.*)

Don't you like chocolate? Sure, you do. Everybody does.

RIVKELE: No, thank you.

SHLOYME: Oh, well. More for me. (*Takes a big bite*) Mmm . . . is that good!

RIVKELE: Please let me go. If my father . . .

SHLOYME: Hey, I hear he's throwing some kind of party for you, is that right?

(*She nods.*)

What's this about a Torah scroll? Old Uncle Jack a yeshi-va *bucha* all of a sudden?

RIVKELE: Please, Shloyme.

SHLOYME: Uh! You know my name!

RIVKELE: Didn't my father tell you never to show your face around here again?

SHLOYME: Hey, you know everything, don't you?

RIVKELE: Papa said you took him for a ride.

SHLOYME (*Amused*): Something like that.

RIVKELE: I won't say anything if you won't.

SHLOYME (*Charmed*): Listen to *you*! Hey, you're a live one, ain't you, Goldilocks. Come on. Have a little candy. Go ahead. I want you to have a bite. It's not gonna kill ya.

(*She hesitates, then slowly takes a bite, her eyes on him.*)

Thatta girl. That wasn't too bad, now was it? Pretty tasty, huh?

RIVKELE: Uh huh.

SHLOYME: See? I wouldn't lie to you. How's Hindl doing?

RIVKELE: Hindl? I don't know.

SHLOYME: She still work down here?

RIVKELE: Uh huh. As far as I know.

SHLOYME: She ever talk about me?

RIVKELE: How am I supposed to know? Now, please, can I go? If my father . . .

(*He pushes her to her feet.*)

SHLOYME: Go. Get outta here. Get your *toochis* back upstairs. Go! Shoo!

(*She heads back up the fire escape, hastily leaving the vestment behind. He finds it.*)

What the hell is this?

*(He covers his face with it and stretches out to take a nap.*
    *Upstairs, Rivkele rushes from her room into the living room,*
*surprising the Indigents who are busily pocketing food. She and*
*the men share a tense moment.)*

FIRST INDIGENT: Jack Chapman sent us.
SECOND INDIGENT: We was invited.

*(Jack, now dressed for the occasion, enters, not realizing what's*
*taking place.)*

JACK: Well! *(Calls)* Sara?! Our guests are here! *(To the Indigents)*
    Welcome, gentlemen, welcome!
FIRST INDIGENT *(Bows obsequiously, covering his theft)*: Mr.
    Chapman! *(Prompts his friend to do the same)*
SECOND INDIGENT: Mr. Chapman, sir!
JACK: Now, now, none of that. You embarrass me, gentlemen.
    The name's Tshaptshovitsh, actually; I was Chapman for
    a while but now I'm using Tshaptshovitsh again, the name
    I was born with. *(Calls)* Sara, come greet our guests!

*(Sara, donning an apron, enters. She tries to hide her disdain for*
*the "guests.")*

SARA: Well, hello!
FIRST INDIGENT: Mrs. Chap— *(Looks to Jack)*
JACK: Tshaptshovitsh. Tshaptshovitsh.
FIRST INDIGENT: Mrs. Tshaptshovitsh.

SECOND INDIGENT: Madame Tshap— (*His friend elbows him for using "Madame"; he corrects himself*) Mrs. Tshaptshovitsh!

FIRST INDIGENT: The lovely lady of the house!

JACK (*To the Indigents*): I see you've already met our Rivkele, the light of our lives.

(*He puts his arm around her shoulder; Rivkele averts her eyes.*)

FIRST INDIGENT: Ah yes, what a girl!

SECOND INDIGENT: Quite a looker!

(*His friend elbows him again.*
*During the following, several more Poor People come down the street and arrive upstairs. They're a rowdy bunch. Ad-lib party talk.*)

POOR MAN: Our generous host! Our lovely hostess! (*Tries to kiss Sara's hand, Sara recoils*)

POOR WOMAN: *Mazel tov.* May the Torah bring you prosperity and happiness.

(*Others concur.*)

JACK: Thank you, thank you. But let's not jump the gun; it isn't mine, not yet. Let's hope and pray. Please, friends, enjoy, help yourselves! (*To Sara*) See? See? And you were worried there'd be no guests.

SARA: You call these "guests"? Where are all the well-to-do neighbors you were talking about?

JACK: They'll be here. (*To Rivkele*) Mingle. Schmooze. These people have come to see you.

RIVKELE: No they haven't . . .

JACK: Go on, sweetheart. Go say hello.

RIVKELE: Must I?

JACK: Yes!

SARA: Do as your father says. Go on.

RIVKELE (*Uncomfortably, to a Poor Man*): Hello, I'm Rivkele. Welcome to our home.

POOR MAN (*Belches, then*): How do you do?

JACK (*To the guests*): How about a little entertainment? Yes? Would you like that? (*The guests respond affirmatively; to Rivkele*) Sing something.

RIVKELE: What?

JACK: Sing for our guests. Go on.

POOR PEOPLE: Oh, yes! Sing! Sing! (*Etc.*)

RIVKELE: What am I supposed to sing?

JACK: Anything.

RIVKELE: I can't . . .

JACK: Of course you can. A little song! A little song is gonna kill you? Sing, darling. (*Announcing*) My Rivkele will sing for you!

POOR PEOPLE: Wonderful! (*Applause, etc.*)

RIVKELE: No, Papa, please . . .

JACK: Go on! What's the big deal? They'll hear your sweet little voice.

RIVKELE: I don't want to, Papa, please don't make me sing for these people . . .

JACK (*Angered, sotto*): Enough of this nonsense! You will do as I say. Now sing!

(*The gathering eggs her on with applause and words of encouragement. She seems utterly miserable as Jack positions her in the middle of the room. He shushes the assembly and gestures to Rivkele to begin.)*

RIVKELE *(Sotto; desperately)*: Mama, I can't think of anything to sing!

*(Sara begins to sing a Yiddish lullaby, gently cuing her daughter. Rivkele sings along, shakily but sweetly. Sara stops singing; Rivkele sings alone.*

*The Orthodox Man emerges from Manke's cubicle and exits as Hindl, a weary hooker in her thirties, enters on sore feet. Not realizing Shloyme is asleep on the chaise, she takes off her shoes, rubs her feet.*

*Upstairs, Rivkele finishes her song and the party applauds her. Jack makes a show of his appreciation. The guests resume eating. We focus on the Poor Women stuffing their faces. Sara winds through with a tray of food and eavesdrops.)*

FIRST POOR WOMAN: What a shame! She's a lovely girl.

SECOND POOR WOMAN: I know. You'd think she was raised in a synagogue, not in a place like this.

FIRST POOR WOMAN: How dreck like those two wound up with such a gem . . .

SECOND POOR WOMAN: God only knows.

JACK *(Approaches, genially)*: So, how's everything?

SECOND POOR WOMAN *(Without missing a beat)*: Ah! We were just saying, what wonderful hosts you are!

JACK: Thank you!

FIRST POOR WOMAN: And that daughter of yours!

JACK: Isn't she something?

FIRST POOR WOMAN: Uh!

SECOND POOR WOMAN: A finer girl you rarely see! You rarely *see* such a girl!

FIRST POOR WOMAN: Even rabbis don't have such daughters.

JACK *(Confidentially)*: You wanna know the truth? I agree with you!

*(They share a laugh. He hands them more food.)*

Here, take, don't be shy, eat, eat, take some more. We wouldn't want you to go home hungry.

POOR PEOPLE: Oh, thank you! Mmm! This is some party! *(Etc.)*

SARA *(Under her breath, to Rivkele)*: This is who he shows off to?

*(Jack taps a glass to get the attention of the gathering.)*

JACK: Ladies and gentlemen. May I have everybody's attention, please.

*(They quiet down.)*

Up until today, I thought we were all alone. Outcasts. Shunned by our neighbors. But now I look around and see all you wonderful friends and neighbors sharing in our *nakhess* and it makes my heart burst in happiness! I am overwhelmed. Thank you for coming, my friends. Thank you! And enjoy! *L'khaim!*

POOR PEOPLE: *L'khaim!*

*(Amid scattered applause, Sara sidles up to him and coaxes him to the stairs.)*

SARA: What is the matter with you?

JACK: Why?

SARA: You talk to these people as if they care about you. They don't care about *you*, they care about your bread and wine, that's what they care about. They'll take your food and then spit at you behind your back! Remember: A *Goy* may be *treyf* but his cash is always kosher.

JACK: I want these people to leave here and tell their friends they were guests of Yankel Tshaptshovitsh and he was a gracious host.

SARA: These people? What do you care what these people think? If we're in the street, they're in the gutter.

*(She moves away with a tray of dishes. He lingers on the stairs thinking about what she's said, looks at his watch, seems worried.*

*We fade out and focus on downstairs: Shloyme, still unseen by Hindl, sits up and watches her looking at herself in the mirror. She catches his reflection and is startled.)*

SHLOYME *(Imitating Jack)*: Why aren't you out on the street?!

HINDL *(Sees him)*: Shloyme!

*(He laughs.)*

You almost gave me a heart attack. What the hell you doing here?

SHLOYME: Ain't you glad to see me?

HINDL: You want the truth?

SHLOYME: Is that any way to talk?

HINDL: I thought you left the neighborhood. Went to Washington Heights or someplace.

SHLOYME: Yeah, but now I'm back.

HINDL: You're just like the clap, you know that? Just when you think you've gotten rid of it . . .

SHLOYME (*Amused*): Hey. Hindleh. Is that how you talk to the man of your dreams?

(*He presents her with the gift-wrapped bundle. She considers it for a moment before rejecting it.*)

HINDL (*Rubbing her feet*): Dreams? I don't know about dreams . . . Nightmares is more like it. Uy, my feet are killing me.

(*He takes over massaging her feet, which she finds suspect.*)

What's this for?

SHLOYME (*Shrugs*): Can't I rub my girl's feet? I missed you.

HINDL: Yeah, sure. You never did this when we were together.

SHLOYME: I never missed you before.

HINDL (*Slaps his hand away*): Two months! Two goddamn months! Not a card, not a word, nothing!

SHLOYME: I'm sorry! Uncle Jack was making life miserable for me downtown. Only the fellas *up*town weren't too crazy about me, either.

HINDL: You never should've sold him that booze. Schmuck.

SHLOYME: I didn't know it was bad. How was I supposed to know?

HINDL: You *should've* known. What kind of way is that to do business?

SHLOYME: What do you want from me? These things happen in business. First you're mad at me for leaving, now you're mad at me for coming back? Hey . . .

*(He touches her breast; she slaps him.)*

Ow!

*(Laughter from upstairs.)*

HINDL: What the hell's going on up there?

SHLOYME: Uncle Jack's having a party. For that precious little girl of his. Boy, I got a good look at her: She's turned into some nice-looking piece. *(Refers to the vestment)* She left her knitting.

HINDL: That ain't knitting; it's embroidery. He's calling himself Yankel now, you know.

SHLOYME: What do you mean?

HINDL: Says he doesn't want to be called Jack Chapman anymore; that was his Yankee name. Now he's Yankel Tshaptshovitsh.

SHLOYME: What, he's getting religious, "Reb Yankel"?

*(They laugh. Pause. He gives her the bundle again. She sits and opens it. It's a pretty shawl. She revels in it for a moment, then stops herself.)*

HINDL: What do you want?

SHLOYME: Why do you always think I want something?

HINDL: Why do you think?

SHLOYME: I came to tell you something.

HINDL: Yeah? Well . . . ? What do you want to tell me?

SHLOYME *(A beat)*: I found a place.

HINDL: What kind of place?

SHLOYME: An apartment. On Rivington Street. Four rooms. Furnished.

HINDL: Four rooms? What do you need all those rooms for?

SHLOYME: What do you think?

HINDL (*A beat; catching on*): Oh . . .

SHLOYME: I'm gonna open the classiest house on the Lower East Side.

HINDL: Is that so. And how you gonna do that all by yourself?

SHLOYME: I'm not. You're gonna do it with me.

HINDL: So, are you asking me, or what?

SHLOYME: Asking you? I'm telling you.

HINDL: Oh. Excuse me: You're telling me. And you're telling me why?

SHLOYME: So you should know.

HINDL: I see. Well, thanks for telling me.

SHLOYME: Ain't you gonna wish me a *mazel tov*?

HINDL: Oh, sure. *Mazel tov* on your new whorehouse. Use it in good health.

SHLOYME: Thanks.

(*Pause.*)

HINDL: You sonofabitch.

SHLOYME: What.

HINDL: You're really not gonna ask me?

SHLOYME: Ask you what?

HINDL: Ask me to *marry* you!

SHLOYME: *Marry* you?! Oh, Jack is gonna love that: Me stealing his girls.

HINDL: He doesn't own me; I'm not their furniture. That Sara looks at me like I'm a—a piece of garbage. So high and mighty she is! Like *she* never had to walk the streets! I'll be the lady of the house. I'll be real good at it, too. You

know I would. I've got a good head for business. I'll run a
tight house for you, Shloym, you know I would.

SHLOYME: Easy, will ya? Slow down! There *is* no house!
There's a vacant four-room apartment! Can't have a house
without girls.

HINDL: I'll get us girls.

SHLOYME: You? What, you're a white slave trader and you
didn't tell me?

HINDL: What if I get you Manke?

SHLOYME: Manke?! You're gonna get me Manke?

HINDL: If I get you Manke . . . She brings in a lot of business,
you know, more than anybody. If I get her for you . . .
Marry me. Make an honest woman out of me, Shloym.

SHLOYME: Too late for that.

HINDL: You gotta get me out of here, Shloym. You gotta take
me with you.

SHLOYME: Take you where? I'm only talking about Rivington
Street!

HINDL: I don't care. I'm dying here, Shloym. (*She kisses him
repeatedly. Sultry, suggestive*) I'll take care of you. You know
how well I take care of you, don'tcha? Don't I take good
care of my man? Huh? Huh?

SHLOYME (*Succumbing*): Aw shit . . .

(*She leads him into her cubicle.
Meanwhile, Sara has rejoined Jack on the landing with a plate
of food.*)

SARA: You should eat something.

JACK: You were right: No one else is coming. No Reb Eli, no
Scribe. We're stuck with the dregs.

SARA: Look: You've got a place to live? Stay there. You've got bread to eat? Eat it. Enjoy. But don't try going where you're not wanted, and don't try being what you're not. Have you forgotten who we are?

JACK: Who are we? Have we robbed anybody? Murdered anybody? I run a business! The need is there, we provide the service. Economics, pure and simple. That's how it works. For this I should be punished? This is America!

*(Downstairs, Hindl and Shloyme:)*

HINDL: Whataya say? Huh, Shloym? Huh?

SHLOYME: I'm starving; I wonder what they got to eat up there.

*(She grabs him by his collar.)*

Hey!

HINDL: I want an answer. If I bring you Manke, will you marry me.

SHLOYME: Knock it off! You're cutting off my circulation!

HINDL: Will you?

SHLOYME: Okay! I'll marry you! I'll marry you!

*(She releases him and kisses him all over.)*

HINDL: Thank you thank you thank you!

SHLOYME *(Overlapping)*: *Now* can we get something to eat?

HINDL: Sure, let's go stuff our faces.

*(Hindl and Shloyme encounter Jack and Sara on the stairs.)*

SHLOYME: "Reb" Yankel!

JACK: Uh! You!

SHLOYME (*Tips his hat*): Sara, you're looking the respectable woman this evening . . .

SARA: Drop dead.

SHLOYME: How long you been holy, "Reb Yankel"? Since lunchtime?

JACK: Get out of here. Now! Go!

HINDL (*Helping herself to food*): Is that any way to treat your old friends?

SARA: Old friends?! Ha!

JACK: *Goniff!* The nerve of you showing your face around here!

SHLOYME: We came to pay our respects. To little Rivkele.

JACK: Yeah? Well, nobody invited you.

SHLOYME: You invite bums in off the street but business associates you throw out?

JACK (*Overlapping ". . . you throw out?"*): "Business associates"?! You call what you do business?!

SARA (*Overlapping ". . . business?!"*): Don't even speak to them. Get them out of here!

HINDL (*Hefts a fork*): Is this real silver?

SARA (*Snatches the fork*): Out of my house. Vermin!

HINDL: The hell with your house. We're gonna have a house of our own.

SHLOYME: Hindl . . .

JACK (*Overlapping; skeptical*): Your own house, is that so?

HINDL: That's right. Shloyme's gonna marry me.

SHLOYME (*To Hindl*): You got a big mouth, you know that?

SARA (*Overlapping*): Marry you?!

HINDL: Why? *That* prize married *you*. (*To Shloyme*) Tell them!

SHLOYME: She's gonna be my girl now, what do you think about that?

SARA: Oh, really! I wish you luck!

JACK (*Overlapping; to Shloyme*): I'm not gonna discuss this with you up here. (*Escorting him*) Downstairs, the both of you, now!

SHLOYME (*Pulling away from him*): Hey! Watch the hands!

JACK: Downstairs! If you have anything to say to me, you say it downstairs. Upstairs, I don't know you and you don't know me.

SHLOYME: I got news for you, Yankel Chapawhozitz or whatever you're calling yourself these days: Upstairs, downstairs, the Devil's the same all over.

JACK: Out of here! Now!

SARA (*Taking food from Hindl*): Don't you have work to do? You barely earn your keep anymore!

HINDL: Oh, yeah? Let's see *you* go downstairs and peddle *your* ass, see how much *you* bring in!

SHLOYME (*To Hindl*): Better yet, tell her to send down little Rivkele.

(*He and Hindl laugh.*)

JACK (*Attacking him*): You sonofabitch! How dare you! How dare you even speak her name! You are scum! Scum!

(*A fight ensues. The remaining guests disperse. During the commotion, Manke emerges from her cubicle downstairs and listens. Upstairs, Rivkele stands in her doorway, fascinated. Jack roughhouses Shloyme down the stairs to the sidewalk and puts a switchblade to his throat.*)

SARA: Oh, my God! Jack!

HINDL: Shloyme!

SARA (*Overlapping; to Jack*): Stop it!

RIVKELE: Mama?

SARA (*To Rivkele*): Into your room!

RIVKELE: Mama, what's happening?

SARA: Now!

(*Rivkele ducks back into her room.*)

JACK (*To Shloyme*): If I ever hear you speak her name again ... If I ever see your face again ...

(*Meanwhile, Reb Eli, a matchmaker and all-around go-between, and Reb Aaron, the Scribe, an ancient, mysterious, pious man, come down the street.*)

ELI (*Entering; overlapping*): Oh, my oh my! Gentlemen! Gentlemen! What's all this?

SARA: Jack! Reb Eli.

(*Jack stops battling Shloyme.*)

JACK: Reb Eli, hello. (*To Shloyme and Hindl, controlling his rage*) Go.

ELI: Shame on you! You should be rejoicing, not fighting.

(*Jack's eyes are on Shloyme and Hindl, who is nursing Shloyme's bloody lip.*)

JACK: Forgive me. I was evicting some riffraff. They were just leaving.

SHLOYME (*Fixing his collar*): Come, Hindleh. I can tell when we're not welcome. So long, "Reb" Yankel. (*To Hindl*) Get a load of who he's taking up with. Next thing you know, he'll be running for mayor.

(*Hindl laughs. They exit brusquely past Eli and the Scribe.*)

JACK: Pardon the intrusion. Please, come upstairs. You open your home to the neighborhood, you're bound to get a few rotten apples. (*A nervous laugh*)

ELI: Yes. Well. (*To the Scribe, making introductions*) Aaron ... this is Mr. Chapman.

JACK: Tshaptshovitsh. Remember?

ELI: Yes, yes, excuse me. Tshap—?

JACK: Tshaptshovitsh.

ELI: Mr. Tshaptshovitsh.

JACK: Hello, sir. Welcome. Welcome to my home.

(*Jack extends his hand which the Scribe pointedly doesn't shake. Jack withdraws his hand in embarrassment.*)

SCRIBE (*To Eli, his eyes on Jack*): This is the man who wants to buy the Torah scroll?

ELI: Yes.

SCRIBE (*Cooly*): Sholem-aleykhem.

JACK: Aleykhem-sholem.

(*Sara bows, steps back respectfully as the Scribe comes forward.*)

Please, sir. Sit down. Sara?

*(Sara sets out a chair for the Scribe.)*

Some schnapps? Hm?

*(The Scribe shrugs, nods. Jack fills glasses, with Sara's help, gives them to the men.)*

ELI: *L'khaim.*
JACK: *L'khaim.*

*(Eli and Jack down their drinks but the Scribe does not, unnerving them. Sara steps forward to brightly offer some food but Jack restrains her.)*

SCRIBE *(To Eli, while looking at Jack)*: This is the man?
ELI: Yes, Aaron, this is the man. He doesn't have a son, so he wants to serve God by purchasing his own handwritten copy of the Torah. *(To Jack)* Isn't that right?
JACK: Yes.

*(Eli prompts him to be more positive.)*

Oh, yes! For my daughter's dowry. I thought if I could buy the one you—
ELI: Just answer yes or no. *(Continuing, to the Scribe)* This is very honorable, no? We must celebrate this in any man.
SCRIBE: Tell me: What sort of man is he?
ELI: What sort of man?
JACK: Well, you see Rebbe—
ELI *(Cutting him off)*: What difference does it make? He's a Jew, is he not?
JACK: True. I'm a Jew.

ELI: An ordinary Jew. If you mean, is he a scholar? No. The answer is no.

JACK: No. No scholar.

ELI: But does every Jew have to be a scholar?

JACK: That's right!

ELI: If a Jew wants to do a *mitzvah*, like this, don't we owe him something? A helping hand at least? Now, come, Aaron, let's drink . . . *(Refills his and Jack's glasses)* *L'khaim*.

JACK: *L'khaim*.

*(Eli and Jack drink; once more, the Scribe does not.)*

SCRIBE: Does he know how to conduct himself with a holy book?

ELI: Of course he knows.

JACK: Of course I know.

ELI: What Jew doesn't know what a Torah is?

JACK: Exactly. I was *bar mitzvah* forty-odd years ago, in Warsaw. A Jew is what I am.

ELI *(Prepares another round)*: *L'khaim, l'khaim* . . . Let us toast. May God grant us better times.

JACK: Better times. *L'khaim*.

*(Jack drinks with Eli. The Scribe does not.)*

SCRIBE: A Torah is a magnificent thing.

JACK: Oh, I know.

SCRIBE: Remember that.

JACK: I do, Rebbe, I do.

ELI: Shh. Listen.

SCRIBE: One handwritten scroll enfolds the entire world. Each Torah is like the very Tablets of the Law that were handed down to Moses from Mount Sinai. Every line, every stroke of the pen, is written in purity and holiness. And where a home has a scroll of the Torah, then God is there, too. So, for that reason alone, it must be kept free of contamination. Do you understand what that means?

JACK (*Terrified by the Scribe's speech*): Yes, Rebbe.

SCRIBE: Do you understand that responsibility?

JACK: Yes, Rebbe, listen, I must tell you something . . .

ELI (*To Jack*): What are you doing?

JACK: I must tell him everything. I must tell him the truth.

ELI (*Quietly, to Jack, trying to save the deal*): No no no . . .

JACK: Rebbe, I am a sinful man . . .

ELI (*Overlapping*): Sh sh sh. (*To Scribe*) Rebbe, the man is a penitent, see?, so we have to help him, right? The Talmud says so. Doesn't it?

JACK: I got caught up in business. I forgot about God.

ELI (*Sotto, to Jack*): Quiet!

JACK: I changed my name. I denied who I was. I tried to hide from God.

ELI: Let me handle this, will you!

JACK: I'm tired of hiding, Rebbe, I don't want to hide anymore.

ELI: What it comes down to is . . .

JACK: I've taken back my name. My Jewish name, the name I was born with.

ELI: What it comes down to is respect. As long as you respect the Torah, and watch your tongue, and be pious and modest, what could go wrong?

SCRIBE: A single word, heaven help us!, one single word could disgrace the Torah, and then a huge calamity might descend on not just you but on all Jews, everywhere!

JACK (*Agitated*): Rebbe . . . Listen . . . I'm not worthy of your presence here, under my roof.

ELI: Don't . . . !

JACK: I have to say this. Rebbe, I am a sinful man.

ELI (*To himself*): Uy.

JACK (*Holding Sara by her shoulders*): *She* is a sinful woman.

SARA: Yankel.

JACK: We don't have the right to even touch a Torah scroll. But there . . . (*Points to Rivkele's room*) In there, Rebbe . . . An angel lives there . . . Let me show you.

(*Jack goes into Rivkele's room, surprising her. He takes her by the hand and leads her into the living room.*)

This is my Rivkele. The scroll is for her, Rebbe, not for me. (*Takes her hands, lovingly examines them*) These hands, Rebbe, look at these hands. These are the purest hands imaginable. (*To Rivkele*) Go, darling, show the rebbe what you're making for the Torah.

RIVKELE (*Panicked but trying not to show it*): What?

JACK: The vestment. Show him.

RIVKELE: Um . . .

JACK: Show him.

RIVKELE: Oh, Papa, must I?

JACK: Yes.

RIVKELE: But . . . it's . . . it's not finished.

JACK: So what? Go get it.

RIVKELE (*Tearfully*): Please, Papa . . . don't make me . . . please don't . . .

SARA (*Urges gently*): Yankel . . .

JACK (*To Rivkele*): Uh, okay, dearest. (*To the men*) She's shy. You see what humility?

(*He takes her hands and displays them for the Scribe.*)

These hands, Rebbe, have embroidered the finest vestment for a Torah I have ever seen. Wait till you see. You will be amazed. My hands won't touch your Torah scroll. (*Points to Sara*) Her hands won't, either. But *these* (*Rivkele's*), *these* hands will. She'll take care of it. And honor it. It will stay in her room. And when she marries, she can take it with her wherever she and her husband may go.

ELI (*To the Scribe*): See? See? Isn't that wonderful?

JACK: "Forget your father," I'll tell her. "Forget your mother. Have pure, decent children of your own." (*Quietly, to Rivkele*) Now, go, sweetheart. Go to your room. (*Kisses her head; smiles, watches as she goes*) Rebbe, *we* are the sinful people. (*Meaning Sara and himself*)

SARA (*Under her breath*): All right, already, Yankel.

JACK: Not her. This is why I went over to the synagogue and went up to this man (*Meaning Eli*), this man who is so wise about other peoples' lives, and I said to him, "Reb Eli, I need your help. I am a sinful man, but how can I protect my daughter from sin? I may be doomed but how can I save her? How can I make sure she gets the decent husband she deserves?" And he said to me, "Have a Torah put it in your house." He told me you had just copied one, for a man who died. Rebbe, that's all I want, that's all I ask. Please, sir. I must have that scroll.

(*Eli confers with the Scribe. Jack and Sara watch expectantly as the old man weighs his verdict.*)

SCRIBE: We will need a *minyan.*

ELI *(Relieved)*: No problem. We'll go to the synagogue, we'll find ten men.

JACK *(Overlapping)*: Thank you, thank you.

ELI *(Refills glasses)*: Now: Good—let's drink. *L'khaim.*

JACK: *L'khaim.*

SCRIBE: *L'khaim.*

ELI: You see, Reb Aaron? Even if a Jew sins, he's still a Jew. A Jewish soul wants the best for his child. *(To Jack)* God loves a penitent, true. But you have to make donations to the scholars.

JACK: Of course.

ELI: If you're not a scholar yourself, then you have to support scholarship. Because *al toyrah oylem oymeyd*: On the Torah rests the whole world. Isn't that right, Reb Aaron? Isn't that the way it is? *(The Scribe nods; to Jack)* Give up your old ways and support scholars.

JACK: Oh, I will, I will.

ELI: Forget the path you've been on and follow a different path.

JACK: I am, I will.

ELI: Do these things and eventually God will forgive you.

JACK: I'm gonna follow a different path, the path that leads to God.

*(Eli puts his arm around Jack, walks him away from the Scribe.)*

ELI: I've made some progress in lining up that bridegroom for your daughter.

JACK: Oh, yes?

ELI: A scholar. Who's going to college!

JACK: You hear this, Sara? College!

ELI: And now that you have a Torah for a dowry?!

JACK: Oh, thank God!

ELI: Come, let's find a *minyan* and rejoice in the Holy Book.

JACK: Wait. You're saying I can walk down the street with men such as yourselves?

ELI: Why not?

JACK *(Moved)*: You're not ashamed to be seen with me?

ELI: Look, if God forgives you, then *we* can certainly forgive you. Isn't that so, Reb Aaron?

SCRIBE *(Shrugs)*: Who can say? Our God is a God of mercy, a God of compassion—but we mustn't forget: He is also a vindictive God, a God of vengeance. *(Looks at the fading light)* Hm, it's getting late. Come, if we're going to synagogue, we must go now . . .

*(The Scribe exits the apartment, starts going down the stairs.)*

JACK: What did he mean by that?

ELI: Don't worry about it. *(To Sara)* You think maybe you can prepare a little something for when we come back?

SARA: Consider it done.

JACK: Reb Eli, I am so grateful. How can I ever repay you?

ELI: Let me tell you about our new scholarship fund.

JACK: Could it be in my name?

ELI: Of course it can. If the donation is sizable enough.

*(They go down the stairs and down the street. Sara primps in front of a mirror and putters as she calls to Rivkele, who is lying dreamily in bed, alone in her room.)*

SARA: Rivkele!

RIVKELE: Yes, Mama?

SARA: The men have gone to get a *minyan*. They'll be back any
minute. Put on your nice blue dress. Hurry.

RIVKELE: Yes, Mama.

*(She gets out of bed. Meanwhile, Manke climbs the ladder of the
fire escape and soon appears at Rivkele's window. Rivkele is ter-
ribly excited to see her but dares not exclaim; Manke slowly
moves toward her as Sara continues speaking from the next room.
The girls hardly take their eyes off each other.)*

MANKE *(Whispers)*: Are you all right?

*(Rivkele nods.)*

I had to see you.

SARA: I can't believe this day has come.

RIVKELE *(Whispers, to Manke)*: You'd better go. My mother . . .

MANKE *(Touches Rivkele's lips to silence her)*: Shhh . . .

SARA: Your father has talked about this day, sweetheart, for so
long. He wants so much for you to have a respectable life.
You do know that, don't you, darling?

RIVKELE: Yes, Mama, I know.

SARA: Reb Eli says it's looking very good for this bridegroom!
But I should keep my mouth shut. *Kinna horee*, I should
keep my mouth shut. Do you need help in there?

RIVKELE: No! I don't need help. *(Her eyes on Manke)* Tell me
about my bridegroom, Mama.

*(Manke helps her out of her party dress and into a more austere
one.)*

SARA: Your bridegroom?! We shouldn't talk about him. It's bad luck.

RIVKELE: Please, Mama, I want to know. What is he like?

SARA: Well . . . he's very special.

RIVKELE: Yes?

SARA: Oh, yes. A treasure.

RIVKELE: A treasure?! Yes!

SARA: A scholar. Very smart. And kind.

RIVKELE: Yes. So kind.

SARA: An honest man. A good provider.

RIVKELE: Where will we live, Mama, my bridegroom and I? Where will we go?

SARA: He'll take you to live in a fine house. Filled with light. With trees all around. And your children—respectable, decent children—will run through the fields, laughing.

RIVKELE: What does he look like, Mama? Is he handsome?

*(Manke takes Rivkele's face in her hands and kisses her passionately on the lips. They caress one another.)*

SARA: Oh, yes! Very handsome. Beautiful, really.

RIVKELE: Yes. So so beautiful.

SARA: Clear, pale skin—white, almost.

RIVKELE: Yes.

SARA: Shiny black hair. And a smile . . . ! Such a smile!

RIVKELE: What about his eyes, Mama. Tell me about his eyes.

SARA: His eyes are dark. But they sparkle. Like jewels.

RIVKELE: Yes! They do! And his hands, are his hands gentle?

SARA: Yes. But also strong.

RIVKELE (*Responding to Manke's touch*): Mmm. Will he touch me and caress my hair? Will he, Mama? Will he tell me I'm pretty?

SARA: Yes, yes, always.

RIVKELE: Will he love me, Mama?

SARA: Will he love you?

RIVKELE: Yes. Will he love me, my bridegroom? Will he?

SARA: Oh, yes. Of course he'll love you. Completely. With all his heart.

(*We hear sung prayers as holy men in black—ten in all, the* minyan, *including Jack, Eli and the Scribe, who holds the Torah, which seems to glow from within—come down the street and begin to go upstairs.*)

Oh, my God! They're coming! He's back with the men! Hurry hurry hurry! They're on their way!

(*Manke and Rivkele share a parting kiss. Rivkele gets into her dress as Manke descends the fire escape ladder. The men file into the upstairs apartment as the curtain falls.*)

# ACT TWO

*A light spring rain. Later that night.*

    *Lights up on the gleaming Torah, now hanging in a cabinet on the wall in Rivkele's room. She is in her nightclothes, dreamily humming while brushing her hair. During the following, she gets ready for bed, turns out her light. Her haunting song continues while Manke comes down the street with a customer walking a few steps behind her. Both are holding umbrellas. She enters the downstairs apartment first; the man follows. He gives her money. They go into her cubicle.*

    *Shloyme and Hindl come down the street arguing.*

HINDL: He said hello! What do you want me to do, ignore him? He's just being friendly.

SHLOYME: Friendly?! That ain't "friendly," that's giving you the eye.

HINDL: You're crazy! I know him from the neighborhood. I walk past his hardware store a dozen times a day.

SHLOYME: I saw the way he looked at you, I saw that look.

HINDL: What look?

SHLOYME: "Well hello there, Hindl."

HINDL: That's just Moish. That's how he talks. He's a character.

SHLOYME: Did you do it with him?

HINDL: *Uy gut*, Shloym, what is the matter with you?

SHLOYME: Did you?

HINDL: What, all of a sudden you're jealous?

SHLOYME: Answer me: Did you screw him.

HINDL: You're nuts, you know that?

*(He grabs her by her arm.)*

SHLOYME: Did you?! Did you?! You did, didn't you!

HINDL: Let go of me!

SHLOYME: Did he pay? Huh? Did he, you stinking filthy whore? Did he?

HINDL *(Finally)*: No!

*(Shloyme tosses her aside; she yelps.)*

SHLOYME: And I said I would *marry* you?! What was I thinking?! What the hell was I thinking?!

HINDL *(Overlapping "What the hell . . .")*: He was nice to me! Don't I deserve someone nice now and then?

SHLOYME *(Overlapping ". . . now and then?")*: I said I'd go into *business* with you?!

HINDL: You'd gone away! How was I supposed to know you were coming back? I thought I was never gonna see you again!

SHLOYME *(Overlapping "I thought . . .")*: I must be outta my mind! We'll go broke! You *give* it away!

HINDL *(Overlapping ". . . outta my mind!")*: *You're* my man, not him. I don't give a damn about him! He says hello, I'll cross the street—

SHLOYME: You're secondhand goods!
HINDL: Please, Shloym, let's not fight. Come on, baby, don't . . .

*(She tries to kiss him; he pushes her away.)*

SHLOYME: Get offa me!
HINDL: I promised you Manke. Remember? You said if I got you Manke . . .
SHLOYME: Get *offa* me, I said!

*(He tosses her aside and storms down the street.)*

HINDL: Shloyme, no!

*(She sobs, her face streaks with mascara. Basha and Reyzl run laughing down the street from the opposite direction, their clothing drenched by the downpour.)*

REYZL: Ooo, I love the rain, don't you?
BASHA: Rain makes me homesick.
REYZL: Yeah?
BASHA: Makes me think of the orchard back home . . . The sound of the rain falling on the leaves . . . My mama, may she rest in peace, her borscht on the stove . . . sorrel and beets and dill. *(Inhales)* I can smell it.
REYZL: I remember the goats *we* had, grazing in the rain. I can smell them, too!

*(They laugh.)*

BASHA: Oh, and all my old friends, my girlfriends, oh God, I miss them. They'd be out dancing in the fields in a rain like this. And I'd be dancing with them, barefoot and drenched, far from the *shtetl*, far from our fathers.

REYZL: Would he get mad, your father?

BASHA: Oh God, would he!

REYZL: Mine, too. He used to come after me with a branch!

BASHA: Oh, no!

REYZL: Caught me with a boy once, hit me so hard, it left a scar. See? (*Shows her arm*)

BASHA (*Winces*): Oooh. *My* father was a butcher. He had all these sharp knives. He didn't like something I did? He'd put a knife to my throat and threaten to stick it in!

REYZL: Oh God!

BASHA: I don't know if he's alive or dead and I don't care.

REYZL: Basha!

BASHA: He wanted me to marry Notke, the other butcher in town. It was all arranged.

REYZL: What was he like?

BASHA: Notke? Uch, he was awful. These big hairy hands, and he always smelled like beef!

(*Reyzl laughs.*)

He did! He was disgusting. The thought of spending the rest of my life with him, those rough hairy hands touching me, stinking of blood . . .

REYZL: Ich . . . so what happened?

(*They enter the brothel. Hindl, still unseen, shields her tear-streaked face.*)

BASHA: I ran away. And came here. To America. My mama didn't want me to be a butcher's wife like her. She gave me every last *shekel* she saved to pay my way.

REYZL: Ohhh . . .

BASHA: The last time I saw her, my boat was pulling away. She ran to the end of the dock, all the way to the end, till there was nowhere left to run . . . (*A faraway voice*) "Goodbye, Basheleh! Find a better life! God be with you!" (*Silence. Saddened*) Some "better life."

(*Reyzl puts her arm around her.*)

Thank God she didn't live to find out what I do.

HINDL: And what's wrong with what we do?

REYZL (*Surprised to see her*): Hindl.

HINDL: Are we any different from the shopgirls? Or the factory girls, or the secretaries? We're all out to earn a buck. We all gotta survive. You think the middle-class wives are any better off? *They* gotta work hard for their keep, too— by making their fat husbands happy.

REYZL: Hey. What's with your face?

HINDL (*Self-consciously*): Nothing.

REYZL: You been crying?

HINDL: No . . . (*Fixing her face in the mirror*) Just the rain.

BASHA (*Still haunted by her mother*): She . . . she comes to me sometimes.

HINDL: Who?

BASHA: My poor dead *mamaleh*, from deep in her grave.

REYZL: You *see* her?!

*(Basha nods.)*

When?

BASHA: At night.

HINDL: What are you talking about?

BASHA: She comes to me, her shroud all torn and tattered, covered in mud . . .

REYZL: Uch! What does she do?

BASHA: She gets into bed with me.

*(Reyzl gasps.)*

And tears at my hair because of my sins, the terrible things I've done.

HINDL *(Spooked)*: I don't like this; I don't like this at all.

BASHA: She rips hair from my head and scratches my face with her nails.

HINDL: Stop it.

REYZL: Does she speak?

BASHA: She cries. She howls in shame . . .

*(Hindl shudders.)*

*(A haunted, faraway voice)* "Basha, how could you!? This is not what I wanted for you! This is not what I wanted!"

HINDL: All right, already! Enough about sins! Enough about ghosts! You're giving me the creeps!

*(Meanwhile, Jack, holding a basket of food, comes downstairs.)*

JACK *(Singsong)*: Hell-o-o!

REYZL (*Quietly*): Oh, no!

HINDL (*To the girls*): What does *he* want?

JACK (*Enters cheerfully*): Well! Good evening, girls.

BASHA: Evening.

JACK: Some night, hm? Any business at all?

(*Basha and Reyzl shake their heads.*)

HINDL: Manke. She's got someone.

JACK: Leave it to Manke. So . . . how are my girls?

REYZL: Don't worry, we're going back out.

BASHA: We just came in to change; we got soaked.

JACK: That's all right, I'm not complaining. You hear me complaining? I didn't come here to yell.

REYZL: No?

JACK: No! I came to tell you girls to call it a night.

BASHA (*Incredulous*): You did?

JACK: Stay in! Keep dry! God forbid you should get a cold.

REYZL: You mean you're not gonna make us walk the streets in the rain?

JACK: No no no. Better you should stay in and keep your health.

BASHA: Yeah? But you always said, don't come back unless it's with a customer.

JACK: That was the *old* Yankel. This is the *new* Yankel.

HINDL: The *new* Yankel, huh.

JACK: That's right: The one who's changing his ways.

HINDL: You mean Yankel, the *mensch*, not Yankel, the pimp?

(*The girls look at one another, expecting the worst.*)

JACK (*With a smile*): You're not gonna get a rise out of me tonight, Hindl. Not tonight. Tonight I begin again. I'm so happy, I could ... dance around the room!

(*He spins Basha, who is aghast.*)

BASHA: Mister ... !
HINDL: What's with *you*?!
JACK: What's with *me*? *God* is with me.
HINDL: *Uy vey.*
JACK: Make fun all you want. Look what I brought you ...

(*He unveils a splendid basket of food. The girls exclaim but hesitate.*)

HINDL: Okay, where's the catch?
JACK: There *is* no catch. My!, you're so suspicious, Hindl! Does there always have to be a catch?
HINDL: Generally speaking ... ?
JACK: Can't I give my girls a little treat now and then? Huh? Look at all this beautiful food going to waste! I want you to have it. Take! Help yourselves!

(*The girls warily help themselves.*)

There you go! Don't be shy.
BASHA AND REYZL: Oh, thank you, mister ... thank you. (*They savor the bread, etc.*)
JACK (*Overlapping "... thank you."*): Uncle. Call me Uncle. No one can say I'm not a good employer. Look at the benefits. There! Now isn't that good?

BASHA AND REYZL: Mmm, yes . . . delicious . . . (*Etc.*)

JACK: Whatever you do, don't tell Sara I gave you. She thinks
I'm too generous as it is. (*To Hindl*) Take. It's only gonna
go bad.

HINDL: I don't take charity. Not from the likes of you.

JACK: Oh, I see. Well, aren't you superior. You don't want my
food? Fine. (*A beat*) Your darling boyfriend around?
Excuse me: Your fiancé.

HINDL: What do you care?

JACK: Give him a *challah*. Tell him it's on me.

HINDL: You gotta be kidding.

JACK: No! I told you: I'm not the same man I was when I woke
up this morning. God has been invited back into my
house. He's there. He's right upstairs. Big changes are happening around here.

HINDL: Oh, yeah, what kind of changes?

JACK: *Big* changes. As soon as I get my Rivkele married
off . . . I'm closing up shop.

HINDL: You're what?!

BASHA (*Overlapping*): What do you mean?

JACK: I'm getting out of the business.

HINDL: What do you mean you're getting out of the business?
You're going straight?

JACK: That's right.

HINDL: Ha. What are you gonna do?

JACK: Taxi medallions.

HINDL: *Taxi* medallions?

BASHA (*Overlapping*): Taxis?!

JACK: Mark my words: Taxis are gonna be the next big thing
in this town. I'm buying a whole fleet's worth.

HINDL: Unbelievable.

BASHA: And what happens to us?!

REYZL: You're kicking us out?

JACK: Nobody's kicking you out.

HINDL: Sure.

REYZL: I *live* here; this is my *home!* The only home I've ever had here!

BASHA (*Overlapping "The only home . . ."*): Where are we supposed to go?

JACK (*Overlapping; calming them down*): Shh shh shh . . . Don't get hysterical.

HINDL (*Overlapping*): What does *he* care? He doesn't give a damn what happens to us.

JACK: Quiet, you! (*To the others*) You think I'd just throw you out on the street? Huh? What sort of man do you think I am?

(*Hindl scoffs.*)

I'll send you off with a few bucks to get you started. A little something, you'll be fine.

REYZL: And do what? How we gonna live?

BASHA (*Overlapping "How we gonna . . ."*): This is all I've ever done; I don't know how to do anything else!

REYZL: Me, either!

JACK: You're young, you'll find husbands.

BASHA (*Tearful*): Who's gonna want me?

JACK (*Soothing*): Basha . . .

BASHA (*Continuous*): What kind of man'll want to marry a girl like me?

HINDL: Shloyme's marrying *me* . . .

JACK: You see that?

HINDL: We're opening up a house of our own. You can come work for us.

JACK: Uh! You see that?!

BASHA (*To Hindl*): Work for *you*? What makes you think I'd want to come work for *you*?

HINDL: Well, the hell with *you*!

REYZL: I'd rather starve to death!

HINDL: The hell with both of you! I offer you a roof over your heads and this is how you talk to me?

BASHA: Screw you!

HINDL (*Continuous*): We'll see how you feel when winter comes and you're freezing your tootsies off and you got no place to go!

BASHA (*Overlapping "... and you got ..."*): Oh, yeah?

JACK (*Overlapping*): Girls, girls! Enough of this! Really, now. You should be ashamed of yourselves. There's a Torah upstairs now. Show a little respect. Now go to sleep and get some rest, all of you. Go!

REYZL: Good night, Uncle.

JACK: Good night. And make sure Manke gets some food. (*He starts to go*)

BASHA: Yes, Uncle. Good night.

HINDL: Hey. Reb Yankel. You forgot something.

(*She balls up Rivkele's vestment and throws it at him. He picks it up.*)

JACK (*Realizes*): Oh, my God ... What is this doing here?!

HINDL: I dunno.

JACK: Did you steal it?

HINDL: No!

JACK (*To Hindl, grabbing her arm*): Did you?! Did you snatch it
upstairs from the party?

HINDL (*Overlapping*): No! Let go of me!

JACK: You stole it when no one was looking!

HINDL: I did not! Stop it! You're hurting me!

BASHA: Leave her alone!

JACK (*Grabs Basha*): Did *you?* Did you sneak upstairs?

BASHA: No!

JACK (*Tosses Basha aside, grabs Reyzl*): Did *you?!*

REYZL: Uncle! Please!

JACK: Then how did it get here? Huh? Magic? Somebody
stole it!

HINDL: Nobody stole it, dear, repentant Uncle.

JACK: What?

HINDL: Somebody left it behind.

JACK: What are you talking about, left it behind?

HINDL: Rivkele! Rivkele left it!

JACK: Rivkele?!

HINDL: Yes, Uncle. Your precious Rivkele. She was down
here!

JACK (*Restrains himself from striking her*): How dare you! How
dare you say such a thing!

HINDL (*Overlapping*): She came down to see Manke!

JACK: What?

HINDL: She and Manke are friends! They're friends! Manke's
been teaching her how to embroider! This is *Manke's*
work! *She* did it.

JACK: That's not true! Rivkele did it! She told me herself!

HINDL: You stupid, blind man! She comes down here! Your
darling daughter!

JACK: Liar!

HINDL: I'm not lying! It's the truth!

JACK: I want you out of here first thing in the morning. You hear me? First thing!

HINDL: With pleasure.

JACK: Now, go! All of you! Go to bed! I want you out of my sight!

*(Reyzl and Basha scurry off to their beds. Jack runs upstairs with the vestment. Hindl lingers in the shadows. Jack bursts into Rivkele's room. She wakens, frightened.)*

RIVKELE: Papa!

JACK: Look what I found downstairs! Look! Look!

*(Sara appears in a robe.)*

SARA *(Overlapping "Look!")*: Jack! What's going on?

JACK *(To Rivkele)*: What was this doing there? Huh? Huh?

RIVKELE *(Crying hysterically)*: Papa, please!

JACK *(Continuous; slapping her with the vestment)*: I want an answer! Have you been going downstairs?! Have you? *(Etc.)*

SARA: Jack, leave the girl alone!

RIVKELE *(Overlapping "Have you . . .")*: Papa, don't! Please, Papa! *(Etc.)*

SARA: The Torah! What is the matter with you?!

RIVKELE: Mama?

SARA: Shhh . . .

*(Sara comforts Rivkele, tucks her back into bed. She leads Jack into the other room. Rivkele listens.)*

JACK: That Hindl, you know what she said? She said *Rivkele's* been down there!

SARA: What?

JACK: Can you imagine?

SARA: Oh God . . .

JACK: That whore! Such lies! I could kill her!

SARA: I have to tell you something.

JACK: It's jealousy, *that's* what it is. Jealousy!

SARA *(Overlapping "Jealousy!")*: Listen to me, Yankel. You're not gonna like this.

JACK: Don't tell me that; I hate when you tell me that.

SARA: Sit down.

JACK: I don't want to sit down.

SARA: All right, *don't* sit down.

JACK: What. Tell me.

SARA *(Sighs)*: This isn't the easiest life we've made for ourselves, you know.

JACK: Yeah, yeah. So?

SARA: All I want is for my family to be happy; I want *you* to be happy, I want *Rivkele* to be happy. Sometimes that means I have to look the other way.

JACK: What are you talking about?

SARA: It's true. Hindl is telling the truth.

JACK: What?

SARA: Manke's been teaching her how to embroider.

JACK: Oh my God.

SARA: Rivkele wanted to learn, so I mentioned that Manke did nice needlework and . . .

JACK: *You* did?!

SARA: I'm very sorry, what's done is done!

JACK: What have I been talking about all these years?! Huh? What have I been saying?!

SARA (*Overlapping "What have I been saying?!"*): They're just girls! Like sisters!

JACK: "Sisters"?! What's the matter with you?! Manke is a whore! You want your daughter talking to whores?

SARA: The girl has no friends! She has no friends! Who does she have?

JACK: She has you and me! She has her family!

SARA: She needs more than us. What world are you living in where things are so simple? She's growing up! She's curious about the world! She's lonely! She goes to school and she comes home to her room! Those are the rules you insist she keep. What kind of life is that?

JACK: What do you want, you want your daughter to end up like you?! Huh? Is that what you want?! Like mother, like daughter?

SARA (*A beat; hurt*): No. God forbid she should end up like me.

JACK: There's already *one* whore in the family, what's another one? Why not?, it's the family business!

(*She raises her hand to strike him but he catches it. Pause.*)

SARA: You made me a whore.

JACK: I "made" you . . . ?

SARA: I was practically a child. No older than Rivkele.

JACK: How did I "make" you? With promises of food in your stomach, clothes on your back? Your teeth were falling out when I found you; you were skin and bones. "Saved" you is more like it.

SARA (*Sarcastically*): *Thank* you, Yankel—is that what you want to hear?—thank you for leading me down the road to prostitution. I can't thank you enough.

JACK: Sara.

SARA: You took my soul—and threw it away!

JACK: We had no choice. Rivkele *has* a choice.

SARA: We had a choice. You had no *faith*.

JACK: Faith? The faith was beaten out of me. I had to survive. Things were gonna be different for *her*. Remember? That was what we wanted. That's what all these years have been about. No mixing between upstairs and downstairs! How many times have you heard me say that? They've gotta be kept separate, like kosher from *treyf*!

SARA (*Ironically*): Today was gonna be a new beginning. Remember?

(*He falls to his knees repentantly and clutches her. Sara, surprised, holds his head against her.*)

(*As if to a child*) What is *this*?

JACK (*Tearfully*): I'm sorry . . .

SARA: Oh, Yankeleh . . .

JACK: I didn't mean what I said.

SARA (*Stroking his hair, skeptically*): No? Sounded to me like you meant *exactly* what you said.

JACK: I say things sometimes . . .

SARA: What, you say you're sorry and that makes everything all right?

JACK: What more can I say? (*Sobbing, his face buried in her*) Forgive me. Please. Please, Sara.

SARA: Shhh. All right. (*A beat*) I forgive you. God help me, but I do. (*Pause*) Come. Let's go to bed.

JACK: Sara, what am I going to do?

SARA: You'll talk to her in the morning. (*Helps him to his feet*) Come, *tateleh.*

JACK (*Standing*): Yes. You're right. I'll talk to her in the morning.

SARA: That's right. In the morning.

JACK (*Going, her arm around him*): I'm only looking out for her own good, Sara.

SARA: I know, I know.

JACK: I want her to have a better life.

SARA: Of course you do.

JACK: A respectable life.

SARA: Yes, yes . . .

(*They exit to their bedroom. Rumble of thunder.*

*Downstairs, Manke emerges from her cubicle in a camisole; her customer dresses and leaves. She goes to the window and inhales the rain-cleansed air. She climbs out of the window and stands in the rain under Rivkele's window.*)

MANKE (*Whispers, calls*): Rivkele! Rivkele!

(*Rivkele hears her, goes to her window. Hindl remains in the shadows, eavesdropping.*)

RIVKELE: Oh, Manke! It's you, it's you, thank God it's you!

MANKE: Have they gone to bed?

RIVKELE: I think so.

MANKE: Did he hurt you?

RIVKELE: No, but he scares me so much. It's all my fault. I went down to find you and Shloyme was there—

MANKE (*Overlapping*): Shhh shhh shhh. It's all right; it doesn't matter. Come down.

RIVKELE: What?!

MANKE: The rain feels wonderful! Come down right now!

RIVKELE: We'll get soaked!

MANKE: So what! Feel how warm the rain is!

RIVKELE: Oh, I would love to ...

MANKE: Do!

RIVKELE: But what if my father ...?

MANKE: The hell with him!

RIVKELE (*Giggles*): Manke!

MANKE: The night is so sweet. We'll dance to spring! (*Spins herself around a puddle*)

RIVKELE (*Torn, considering it*): Oh ... I don't know what to do ...

MANKE: Rivkele ...!

RIVKELE: I can't. I mustn't.

MANKE: Stop saying that! Or I'll shout your name and wake up the whole neighborhood!

RIVKELE: Shhh! What if he catches us?

MANKE: What if he does? We have nothing to lose! Our secret is out!

RIVKELE: Yes! You're right. Wait ...

(*She goes to her bed and props up her pillows to make it look like she's sleeping, then returns to the window.*)

Oh God ... I can't believe I'm doing this ...

(*She climbs down the fire escape ladder in her bare feet.*)

MANKE: Yay!

RIVKELE: Ooo, it *is* warm!

MANKE: I told you!

(*Manke takes Rivkele's hands and together they gaily swing around. Their laughter subsides. Manke strokes Rivkele's wet hair and face.*)

(*Gently*) Close your eyes. Feel it? Feel how nice that is?

RIVKELE: Mmm.

MANKE: Let the rain wash away your sadness. Doesn't that feel good?

RIVKELE: Oh, yes!

MANKE: And breathe it in.

(*They inhale together.*)

Do you smell how sweet it is?

RIVKELE: Yes!

MANKE: Who would believe the city night could smell so sweet?

RIVKELE: Oh! My heart.

MANKE: What.

RIVKELE: Feel it. It's pounding.

(*Manke puts her hands on Rivkele's chest.*)

MANKE: Ooo, yes. Your heart is pumping so fast.

(*Silence as she slowly caresses Rivkele's breasts.*)

Your skin is so cool under my hands . . . like cool white snow . . .

*(Rivkele's teeth chatter.)*

Oh, my darling, you're shivering. Come, let's go inside . . .

*(As Manke helps Rivkele back inside, Hindl hides behind the drape of her cubicle and listens. Manke sits Rivkele down on the sofa, gets a towel and a blanket.)*

RIVKELE: I feel so cold all of a sudden . . .

MANKE *(Wrapping her in a blanket)*: Here . . . *(Sits with her)* Cuddle with me. That's right. Snuggle up close. Feel how warm I am?

RIVKELE: Oh, yes.

MANKE: You hold me, and I'll hold you. There.

*(They do.)*

Better?

RIVKELE: Oh, yes. I love how you hold me. No one ever holds me like this.

MANKE: Me, neither.

RIVKELE: No? But all those men . . .

MANKE *(A laughable notion)*: Those men.

*(Rivkele strokes Manke's hand.)*

RIVKELE: I love your hands.

MANKE *(Takes it away; self-conscious)*: I hate how they look.

RIVKELE *(Taking hold of Manke's hands)*: Oh, no, they're so long and sleek and warm.

*(Manke strokes her own face with Rivkele's hair, inhaling its scent.)*

MANKE: Mmm ... Your hair smells so clean. Like the rain. So fresh, so soft. Let me fix your hair, like a bride. *(She begins to)*

RIVKELE: Ooo, yes!

MANKE: You be the bride. A lovely young bride. And I'll be the bridegroom, your new husband. All right?

RIVKELE: Yes!

MANKE: The night of the wedding: The celebration is over. All the guests have gone home. We're sitting at the table with your mama and papa. And—wait! It's getting late. Your parents go off to bed. We're all alone.

*(Rivkele mock-gasps.)*

The nervous bride and her bridegroom. And I sit closer to you, as close as can be. And we hug. Like this.

*(They hug.)*

Ooo, yes! Tight, tight, as tight as can be. And I kiss you. Like this.

*(She kisses Rivkele.)*

And we blush, both of us. And we go to your bed, now our marriage bed, and we lie there, the two of us, side by side, and no one sees, no one knows, and no one cares, for we're married now, just a bride and her bridegroom, and we fall asleep in each other's arms, like this, *(Gets on top of her)* forever and ever and ever ...

*(Hindl comes out of her cubicle, feigning surprise at seeing them.)*

HINDL: Oops! Pardon me!

*(Manke and Rivkele sit up, mortally embarrassed.)*

MANKE: Hindl! What are you doing sneaking up on us?

HINDL: I wasn't sneaking, I was coming out to look at the rain.

MANKE: The rain stopped. Go back to bed.

HINDL: Gee, I knew you girls were friendly, but . . .

MANKE: We were only playacting.

HINDL: Oh, sure. Playacting.

MANKE: Mind your own business.

RIVKELE: Please don't tell my father. If he finds out I was down here . . .

HINDL: Boy, he's got some temper, doesn't he! You should've seen him before. I might just go upstairs right now . . .

RIVKELE: Don't! Please!

MANKE: Why don't you leave us alone?

HINDL: All right. I was gonna tell you something I thought you might find interesting but if you don't want to hear it . . .

MANKE: What.

HINDL *(Singsong)*: Good ni-ight!

MANKE: Hindl! What.

HINDL: Okay, you twisted my arm. What if I told you . . . Jack was shutting down the business?

MANKE: He is not.

HINDL: Yes he is. You think I would lie about something like that?

RIVKELE: It's true; I heard him talking about it.

MANKE: When's this supposed to happen?

RIVKELE: Soon. After my wedding.

MANKE: Oh God.

RIVKELE: It's good news, isn't it?

MANKE: No.

RIVKELE: Why?

HINDL *(Overlapping)*: What's so good about it? Think about it, *mameleh*: If he shuts this place down where does that leave you and Manke?

RIVKELE: I'll still be upstairs and she'll still be downstairs.

MANKE: No . . .

HINDL *(Overlapping)*: Not if she's booted out and you're some-one's little wife.

RIVKELE: Oh God . . .

MANKE: She's right.

RIVKELE: I hadn't thought about that.

HINDL: You're not gonna be able to hop the fire escape and see her anymore.

RIVKELE: Oh, Manke . . . What are we going to do?

MANKE: I don't know.

HINDL: Well, I know what *I'm* doing.

MANKE: What?

HINDL: Getting the hell out of here. Before he throws me out.

RIVKELE: And going where?

HINDL: Someplace new. Someplace safe. That your father doesn't know from. Or your mother. Where there's no more hitting. No more yelling.

RIVKELE: Where is this place?

HINDL: Not far. A few blocks away. But it might as well be the moon.

MANKE: Okay, Hindl. What's the story?

HINDL: You wanna know the story? Shloyme's gonna marry me. *That's* the story.

RIVKELE (*Overlapping*): Hindl, that's wonderful!

HINDL: I never thought he'd ask me, but he did.

MANKE: What does Shloyme have to do with this?

HINDL: He found us a place. Of our own. On Rivington Street. Plenty of room for everybody.

RIVKELE: For everybody?

HINDL: Yeah, for you, too, baby.

MANKE: Oh, I see . . .

RIVKELE: What. I don't understand.

MANKE: She means a place like this. No way on earth would I take you to a place like this.

HINDL: You want to be together, don't you?

RIVKELE: Yes!

MANKE: But not like that. I would never do that to you. Never.

HINDL: So how you gonna be together? Huh? He'll do everything he can to keep you apart. You know he will.

RIVKELE: I'd die if I couldn't see you anymore . . .

MANKE: This is no kind of life for someone like you. This is no life for *anybody*.

RIVKELE: And what kind of life am I looking at now?, living under my father's roof, married off to a man I've never even met?! I want to be with you. I have to be with you. (*She cries*)

MANKE: I won't let you throw yourself away. You hear me?

RIVKELE: Yes.

MANKE: Not for any man. Not for any reason.

(*Manke holds Rivkele tightly.*)

HINDL: All right, enough already, girls. Come, if we're gonna go, let's go.

*(Hindl gets a suitcase and starts packing.)*

RIVKELE: You mean now?!

MANKE *(Overlapping)*: Tonight?!

HINDL: Yeah! I'm outta here tonight. You coming with me, or what?

MANKE: This will change everything. Nothing will be the same after this.

RIVKELE: Let's do it! Let's have an adventure!

MANKE: An adventure?

RIVKELE: Yes! You and me!

HINDL: Thatta girl! Let's get out of here.

RIVKELE: Like this? *(Meaning her attire)* I can't go like this. I have to go back up.

HINDL: No, no, forget about your clothes.

RIVKELE: I just need to pack a few things.

HINDL: Too risky. What if your father hears you?

MANKE: She's right. Forget it.

HINDL: You'll wear *our* clothes.

RIVKELE: *Your* clothes?!

MANKE: Yeah! Let's see, what do I have for you . . . *(She goes through a rack of garments)*
Try this . . .

*(Manke gives Rivkele a dress which she puts on with pleasure.)*

RIVKELE: Ooo! I love it! It feels so silky.

HINDL *(Applying lipstick)*: I'm not gonna miss this place, that's for sure. Not for one minute.

*(She starts applying lipstick to Rivkele's mouth.)*

Here, kid . . . Pucker up.

MANKE (*Stopping her*): No, don't!

RIVKELE: It's okay. I want to see.

(*She lets Hindl finish. Hindl takes her to a mirror.*)

HINDL: There! How do you like that?! Don't you look pretty.

RIVKELE (*Looking at herself and Manke in the mirror*): What do you think, Manke? You think I look pretty?

MANKE (*Rueful*): Yes. Very pretty.

HINDL: Here, try these shoes. Do they fit?

RIVKELE (*Puts them on*): Yes! Good enough!

HINDL: Good! Now: What you need is a hat!

(*Hindl puts a hat on Rivkele's head. Rivkele admires herself in the mirror. Hindl wraps her boa around Rivkele with a flourish.*)

Ladies and gentlemen . . . Miss Clara Bow!

(*Rivkele and Hindl laugh. Manke does not. Their laughter subsides. Rivkele watches Manke pack in silence.*)

RIVKELE: Manke?

MANKE (*Smiles*): Come. We should go.

(*She clicks shut her suitcase and slips her arm through Rivkele's. The three of them begin to exit.*)

HINDL: You won't be sorry. Things'll be different with Shloyme and me. I promise: A whole new world. Wait till he sees who I'm bringing home!

(*Rivkele lingers to take a final look at her building. Manke takes her hand and they run off together.*

*Lights shift. The dead of night. Upstairs: Jack, in a robe, unable to sleep, enters the living room. Restless, he pours himself some wine, sits, thinks.*

*Downstairs: a shriek. Basha, wraithlike in her nightclothes, comes out of her cubicle in an agitated dream state.*)

BASHA: Mama?! Don't hurt me, you're hurting me! . . .

(*Reyzl comes out of her cubicle, comforts Basha.*)

REYZL: Basha . . . Shhh . . . You're dreaming . . .

BASHA: Please, Mama . . . Stop!

REYZL: Wake up!

BASHA (*Wakens with a start*): Oh God . . . Reyzl . . . It was my poor dead mama again . . .

REYZL: I know.

BASHA: Howling and weeping and covered with thorny prickles . . . scratching my face, pulling my hair.

REYZL: Shhh . . .

BASHA (*Haunted voice*): "For this I saved you? For this?" Oh God, I've shamed her so . . .

(*She sobs in Reyzl's arms.*)

REYZL: Poor Basha. Try to sleep. Come, *mamaleh*, I'll tuck you back in. Shhh . . .

(*She leads Basha back to bed. Upstairs, Jack quietly enters Rivkele's room and approaches the cabinet housing the Torah. It seems to glow from within.*)

JACK (*Whispers, to the scroll*): Hello, God. It's me, Yankel Tshaptshovitsh. Welcome to my home. God, you see everything. You know everything I do. If you want to punish me, punish me. But the innocent girl who sleeps here—this angel—doesn't know the meaning of the word "sin." Have pity on her. Amen. (*Sits, whispers gently to the form lying in bed*) Rivkele? I don't want to wake you. I just want to be near you.

(*He pulls up a chair and sits.*)

I used to sit by your cradle while you slept, just to listen to you breathe. I couldn't believe the perfect little miracle God gave to two sinners! You are not the work of a vengeful God, my darling.

(*A beat.*)

I had to find my way by myself, on the street. A greenhorn in America, this scrawny orphan. What did I have? I had nobody; I had nothing. Just my wits. But you, my precious, you're gonna have the life in America we only dreamed about. You, and your children, and their children. Yankel's children. You'll live the dream.

(*A beat.*)

(*More hurt than anger*) So, when I find out you've been going downstairs when I told you never to go downstairs ... When I find out you're making friends with the wrong sort of people ... and lying to me! Sweetheart! Is it any wonder I get upset? I'm better now. I had a talk with your mother. I've calmed down. We'll talk in the morning. Everything will be all right.

(*He reaches for "her" and is shocked to find pillows where he thought she lay. He flings off the blanket and shouts in horror:*)

Oh my God! NO!!!

(*Sara hurries from her room into Rivkele's bedroom.*)

SARA: Jack . . . Jack, what is it?
JACK (*Shouts wildly*): You see your daughter?! Hm? Hm?

(*He throws Sara down onto the bed.*)

SARA: What do you want from *me*?!
JACK: You were too easy on her! You said I was too hard, but *you* . . . !
SARA: How dare you blame me! It was bound to happen! Sin is right down the stairs, Jack— (*Mocking*) "Yankel!" Right down the stairs!

(*He storms out of the apartment and down the stairs.*)

JACK (*Shouts*): Rivkele?!

(*Jack tears into the brothel, pulls Reyzl and Basha out of their beds, manhandles them. They're terrified.*)

Where is she? Hm? Where is Rivkele? Is she here? Is she hiding?

REYZL: I don't know!

JACK (*To Basha*): Do *you*?

BASHA: No! Let go of me! You're hurting me!

(*He releases her, pulls open the drapes exposing the empty cubicles.*)

JACK: Up! Everybody up! Manke! Hindl!

(*He sees evidence of packing. It dawns on him.*)

Oh, my God . . . (*To the others*) Where are they?! Where did they go!

REYZL: We don't know! We were sleeping!

BASHA: We're not their keepers!

JACK (*Shouts*): Sara? Sara?

(*He runs out, encounters Sara on the stairs.*)

SARA: Did you find her? Is she there?

JACK: No! She's gone! She went with them!

SARA: With who?

JACK: Manke's gone, and so is Hindl! She ran away! Your precious daughter! She ran away! With those whores!

(*He rampages around his living room, tossing furniture around, breaking glassware, etc. Sara and the girls huddle together on the stairs and listen in horror.*)

BASHA (*Frightened*): What's happening?

SARA: God help us! I don't know.

BASHA: It's my mother's revenge!

SARA: Go find Reb Eli. Tell him something terrible has happened. Tell him we need his help. We can't have a wedding without a bride. Hurry!

*(Reyzl and Basha don coats and exit. Sara goes back upstairs to find Jack disconsolate and the apartment in shambles. She begins to pick up the pieces.)*

Our daughter has run away, but must you destroy our home too?

JACK *(Quietly)*: What difference does it make? It's all shit. *(A mournful wail)* Rivkele!

SARA: Listen to you! So she's run away! What seventeen-year-old girl hasn't done that?!

JACK: What can I do? There's nothing I can do!

SARA: Go out there! Ask around! Ask the scum you know who make their lives in the gutter! Ask *them* if they've seen your daughter!

JACK: I can't. I can't move my legs. It doesn't matter anymore. Nothing matters. God doesn't want it. He doesn't want it . . .

SARA: *God* doesn't want it? *You're* the one who doesn't want it!

*(She puts on a coat.)*

JACK: Where you going?

SARA: To the streets! If you want to sit here eating your *kishkes* out, fine! I'm going out to look for her!

*(Sara hurries downstairs and exits.
Lights shift. Minutes pass. Just before dawn.*

*Eli rushes up the street and finds Jack upstairs, sitting amid the wreckage.)*

ELI *(Entering)*: Oh my God! Look at you! Look at this place!

JACK *(Muttering)*: Eli, Eli . . . she's gone, Eli. My Rivkele. She's left me.

ELI: Pull yourself together . . .

JACK: She ran away with whores.

ELI: Quiet. Don't speak that way.

JACK: It's true, Eli. The marriage I wanted for her. The future. God doesn't want it.

ELI: Shhh!

JACK *(Overlapping)*: He doesn't want it. It isn't meant to be. *(Wails)* Rivkele! . . . Rivkele! . . .

ELI: What is the matter with you?! You want the whole world to hear? Things like this are best kept private.

JACK: I don't care who hears. My daughter is gone. No more daughter. Rivkele! *(Breaks down sobbing)*

ELI: Enough. You're acting like a crazy man.

JACK: I am crazy. Crazy to believe that my faith would not be mocked. She's gone to the Devil, I just know it.

ELI: Stop it. That isn't true.

JACK: Yes. I know what happens out there. She'll feel . . . temptation.

ELI: Yankel!

JACK: She will. And once it starts to grow inside her . . .

ELI: Uy uy uy.

JACK *(Continuing)*: Once it starts, she won't know how to fight it. She'll surrender. Just like the rest of us sinners.

ELI: All right, now stop that right this minute.

JACK: If only she had died before her time . . .

ELI: What kind of nonsense is *that* now?!

JACK: If she had died, at least I would have known that I buried a pure child. But now . . . ?

*(Eli takes Jack by the hand into Rivkele's room, stands before the scroll.)*

ELI: Come. Let us pray!

JACK: What's the point? He doesn't hear me. He hasn't heard me all along.

ELI: Don't say that! Pray to Him! Pray for His forgiveness!

JACK *(To the scroll)*: Show me! What kind of God are you?!

ELI: Yankel!

JACK: Perform a miracle! Go on! Send down a fire to consume me!

ELI: Enough!

JACK *(Continuing)*: Open up the ground and let it swallow me up!

ELI: Enough with that!

JACK: Please please please, God, please protect my child. Send her back to me as pure, as innocent as she was. Otherwise I say that You are no God at all!

ELI *(Aghast)*: You mustn't speak this way!

JACK *(Continuing)*: You are vindictive! No better than a man!

ELI: That is blasphemy! Beg His forgiveness! Pray with me! Now!

*(Eli leads Jack in prayer.*
    *Lights shift. Minutes pass. Sara hurries down the street with Shloyme.)*

SHLOYME (*On the move*): This better be good, dragging me out of my poker game . . .

SARA: What do *you* care, you were losing. Come, I'll give you some schnapps . . .

(*She enters the brothel, pours drinks.*)

SHLOYME (*Hesitates*): Uh-uh, no thanks, I don't want to run into your husband.

SARA: Don't worry about *him* . . . He's fast asleep.

SHLOYME (*Enters*): I liked him better *before* he found God.

SARA (*Hands him a drink*): You and me both. L'khaim.

(*They drink.*)

Got a cigarette?

(*He gives her one, holds her hand as he lights it for her.*)

SHLOYME: You know? You must've been some looker.

SARA: Yeah? Well, you're right.

SHLOYME: Even now. You're not bad.

SARA: Gee, that's some compliment coming from you— seeing what sophisticated taste in women you have. I mean, really, Shloyme: Hindl?

SHLOYME: Oh, come on, Hindl's not so bad.

SARA: No?! She's bounced around every flop-house on the Lower East Side, that girl! She's all used up! You—you're young, you're smart, you're not bad-looking . . .

SHLOYME: Gee, thanks.

SARA: You could get any girl you want! A girl from a good family, even. Have a little self-respect! Don't sell yourself short!

SHLOYME: How come you're so interested in *me* all of a sudden?

SARA (*Her hand inching up his inner thigh*): I just hate to see all
that potential go to waste.

SHLOYME: What'd you want to talk about anyway?

SARA: Business.

SHLOYME: Yeah? So talk.

SARA: I want you to do something for me.

SHLOYME: Yeah? And what you ever do for me?

SARA (*Seductively*): What would you *like* me to do? Huh? I'll
do an-y-thing you want.

(*He removes her hand and backs away. She takes cash out of her
purse.*)

SHLOYME: What's all that?

SARA: Investment for the future. Three or four hundred—I'm
not sure, I haven't counted it lately.

SHLOYME: What're you doing walking around with all that
money?

SARA: You can have it—it's yours.

SHLOYME: What do you mean, it's mine? How's it mine?

SARA: Just tell me where my daughter is.

SHLOYME: Your *daughter*?! How'm I supposed to know? Ain't
she tucked away upstairs in her bed?

(*During the above, Hindl runs up the street and enters the brothel.*)

HINDL: I did it, Shloym! I got you the girls! Just like I said.
Manke and Rivkele, too!

SHLOYME (*Comprehending*): Oh . . .

SARA (*Overlapping; to Hindl*): Where is she?! Huh?! Where'd you take her?!

HINDL: Damned if I tell *you*!

SARA: Bitch! (*To Shloyme*) Is opening a house with a broken-down whore the best you can dream about? Is it?

HINDL (*Overlapping "Is it?"*): Screw you!

SARA: You can do anything. This is America. This'll help you get started.

HINDL: That Rivkele's a gold mine. That face, that little body of hers? The men are gonna be all over her—they're gonna be lining up!

(*Sara thrusts the money at him.*)

SARA: Take it. Where is she? What's the address?

HINDL: Don't, Shloym. The girl's worth a lot more than a wad of cash.

(*Sara takes off her earrings.*)

SARA: Take these, too. Hock 'em. That's a couple hundred right here.

(*Shloyme is considering it.*)

HINDL (*To Shloyme*): Don't. We're so close! We're in business, baby. We're all set. We're getting married! Let's do it today!

SARA (*Overlapping*): You don't need *her*.

HINDL: Yes, you do. You love me! I know you do!

SARA: Here's your ticket, right here . . . right in my hand . . .

HINDL: Don't listen to her, Shloym . . . We're better than her.

*(Shloyme and Hindl look at one another.)*

SHLOYME *(While looking at Hindl)*: Two-eleven Rivington Street.

*(He takes the jewelry. Hindl cries out.)*

*(To Sara)* Come, I'll walk you.
SARA: Thanks.

*(Sara walks past Hindl who stands crumpled in the doorway.)*

SHLOYME *(To Hindl)*: Hey. Let's face it: It's for the best.

*(Hindl slaps his face. Shloyme and Sara exit down the street. Hindl, depressed, goes into her cubicle and draws the drape. Upstairs, Eli paces while Jack sits despondently.)*

ELI: All is not lost. We can still save this match. When I talked to the boy's father, I dropped a few hints that the bride's family, well, that maybe she doesn't come from the best of families and he didn't bat an eye. He still wants to meet you. I said I would bring him around first thing this morning.

JACK: This morning?! But how can he come?! There is no match! I have no daughter!

ELI: He doesn't have to meet the girl. He wants to meet *you*. We can buy some time. Now, please, get dressed and let's clean up this mess; we can't have it looking like this.

*( Jack dresses while Eli picks up.*
*Lights shift. Minutes pass. Morning.*
*Sara comes down the street with her arm around Rivkele who is wrapped in a large shawl.)*

SARA: Thank God I found you. You had yourself a misadventure, that's all. What child doesn't get into mischief every now and then?

RIVKELE: Where's Manke?

SARA: Forget about Manke. I don't think you'll be seeing Manke anymore. Now: When your father asks questions, don't say any more than you have to. Remember: The fewer words the better.

RIVKELE: Mama . . .

*(At the steps, Sara fixes Rivkele's appearance.)*

SARA: Now, let's see . . . if only I had a comb. I'd fix your hair in braids.

RIVKELE: Leave it! I don't want my hair in braids.

SARA *(Taken slightly aback)*: All right. We'll leave it.

RIVKELE: Please don't make me go up there.

SARA: He's not gonna hurt you. I promise. I won't let him.

RIVKELE: You *always* let him.

SARA *(Taken further aback)*: Rivkele!

RIVKELE: It's all right, Mama, I know: We all take what we can get.

SARA: Hate me all you like . . .

RIVKELE: I don't hate you.

SARA: Hate your father. But don't—I beg you—don't destroy your future out of spite. This marriage . . .

RIVKELE: Mama . . .

SARA: It's a real opportunity! A way out! We can still make it
happen! No one has to know *anything*! Come, sweetheart,
whatever you do, don't make him mad.

*(They go upstairs. Eli sees them approach from the top of the stairs.)*

ELI: Thank God! They're here!

JACK *(Still dazed)*: What?

ELI: Your wife and child. See? God did help you. He punishes
but He also heals. *(To Rivkele)* Hello, dear. Thank God
you're home safely. You had us all so worried there for a time.
*(To Jack)* Now: Before anything else should go wrong, let me
quick find the father of the bridegroom and finish the
deal. Pay the dowry right away, whatever it is, today. And
no hemming or hawing about the wedding, either.

JACK *(To Rivkele, but not looking at her)*: I just want to know one
thing. And I want the truth.

ELI: Leave it alone, Yankel. Just thank God for her return and
leave it alone.

SARA: He's right, Yankel.

JACK: Just the truth. That's all I ask.

ELI: God will help and, in time, everything will work itself out.
*Tshuvah, tefilah, tzedaka*: Penitence, prayer and charity. *(To
Sara)* You might want to tidy up a little bit more.

SARA: Yes; I will.

ELI: And cheer up, everybody. Smile. You wouldn't want any-
one to think something was wrong. I'll be back.

*(Eli goes down the stairs, exits. Jack, Sara and Rivkele stand in
silence, the girl's face still obscured by her shawl. Jack approaches
her. She flinches.)*

JACK: I only want to see your face. Let's see . . .

(*He gently reveals her face; she averts her eyes.*)

There you are, my darling. (*To Sara, hopefully*) See?

(*Sara nods.*)

It's still the same girl. Isn't it?
SARA: Yes, it is.
JACK (*To Rivkele*): Come. Sit with me.

(*Rivkele doesn't move.*)

Don't be shy.
RIVKELE: I'm not shy.
JACK: Sit with me, I said.
RIVKELE: No, Papa.
JACK: No?
SARA: Your father wants you to sit with him.
RIVKELE: And I told him I don't want to. (*Looking at Jack defiantly*) No, thank you. I'll stand.
JACK (*To Sara*): What kind of talk is this? She runs away from home and she comes back with a mouth?
RIVKELE: Not a mouth. Just a tongue.
JACK: Well! Well!
SARA: Yankel, don't. We're all tired.
RIVKELE: Not me. I'm wide awake.
JACK (*To Rivkele*): I have one question. Only one. But I want the truth. You understand?
RIVKELE: Papa . . .
JACK: *Do you?*

RIVKELE: I understand.

JACK (*Pauses; gently*): Tell me you're the same girl who left here last night. The same, pure girl. That's all I want to hear. You can tell me, darling.

RIVKELE: I don't know!

JACK: You don't *know*?! What do you mean, you don't know?!

RIVKELE: What is "pure"? I don't know what it means!

JACK: That's ridiculous! Look me in the eye and tell me. Tell me the truth.

(*Rivkele looks at him but doesn't say anything. Silence. He unravels her shawl, unveiling her garish dress.*)

Oh my God!

(*Jack puts his fingers around her neck. Rivkele is not afraid.*)

SARA: Don't!

JACK (*To Rivkele*): If I had done this, long ago . . .

SARA: Jack!

JACK (*Continuous, ignoring Sara*): If I had twisted your neck off before you grew up . . .

SARA: Oh my God, Jack . . .

JACK: If I had cut off your breath . . . Maybe we all would've been better off.

SARA: Stop it!

JACK (*Tearfully*): *Look* at you!

RIVKELE: Go ahead. Do it now. I don't care.

SARA: Rivkele! (*Pulls her away from Jack*)

RIVKELE (*Continuous, to Jack*): Cut off my breath, just as you've been suffocating me all my life!

(Sara gasps.)

JACK: What are you talking about, suffocating.

SARA: Leave it alone, leave it alone, Jack . . .

RIVKELE (Overlapping): You kept me locked in my room!

JACK: Locked in your room?!

RIVKELE: You made me your prisoner!

JACK: Darling! I was protecting you!

RIVKELE: From what?

JACK: From evil! From sin! It's a sinful world out there! You're just a child!

RIVKELE: No! Not just a child! Not anymore!

JACK (A beat): What do you know?

RIVKELE: Everything! I know everything!

(Meanwhile, Eli and the Prospective In-Law, the father of the would-be bridegroom, come hurriedly down the street and mount the stairs.)

ELI (Animatedly, while walking): Yes, yes, he's very eager to meet you. And his daughter! Such a fine girl and a pretty one! A scholarly son-in-law he's after and he'll support them the rest of their lives.

PROSPECTIVE IN-LAW: Ah, good, very good.

(They enter the apartment. Eli feels the chill in the air.)

ELI: Well! Here we are! Aren't we lucky! The entire Tshaptshovitsh family . . . The mother of the bride . . .

PROSPECTIVE IN-LAW: How do you do?

SARA: How do you do.

ELI: The father of the bride . . .

PROSPECTIVE IN-LAW *(To Jack)*: Sir . . .

ELI: And the lovely Rivkele.

JACK *(Bitterly)*: Yes sir, a finer, chaste maiden you will never see.

ELI: Yes, well. *(To the Prospective In-Law)* Isn't she something? Can you imagine a better match for your boy?

*(The Prospective In-Law nods.)*

JACK *(Takes Rivkele's hand brusquely)*: Such a fine, chaste girl I have, no?

RIVKELE: Papa . . .

JACK *(Maniacally)*: And what fine, chaste children she will have! *(To Sara)* Right? Oh, what a future! What a bright future! The *years* we dreamed of this . . . Her mother will lead her to the wedding canopy . . . in the whorehouse!

*(Screams, shouts, cries—a cacophony.)*

PROSPECTIVE IN-LAW: What? What did he say?

ELI *(Overlapping)*: Oh, no, have you gone crazy?

JACK: Down to the whorehouse! Go! Get out of here, all of you!

RIVKELE: Papa!

*(Jack pushes Rivkele toward the stairs.)*

JACK: You're all whores! *(To Sara, evicting her)* You, too!

SARA: Jack! No!

JACK: Go! Everyone! Downstairs!

PROSPECTIVE IN-LAW *(Overlapping)*: What's going on here?

ELI: He's mad!

JACK (*To Eli*): You can go, too! Go on! Go! Good-bye!

ELI: You fool! You crazy fool!

JACK: Wait! Before you go . . .

(*He rushes into Rivkele's room, takes the scroll.*)

ELI: Don't throw it all away! Think about what you're doing!

(*Jack wields the Torah over his head, as if he is about to throw it at Eli.*)

Remember God, Yankel! Remember God!

(*Jack instead thrusts the Torah into Eli's arms.*)

JACK (*To Eli*): Take it with you! I don't need it anymore!

(*Eli and the Prospective In-Law leave with the scroll. Manke runs on and sees Rivkele, who breaks away from Sara and goes to her. Sara watches as the girls exit together, Manke holding Rivkele. Sara, shattered, resignedly trudges back upstairs to join Jack in the ruins of their home.*

*Downstairs, Hindl robotically applies lipstick before setting out for another day of walking the streets.*

*Lights fade.*)

END OF PLAY

DONALD MARGULIES received the 2000 Pulitzer Prize for Drama for *Dinner with Friends* (Variety Arts Theatre, New York; Comedie des Champs-Elysees, Paris; Hampstead Theatre, London; Actors Theatre of Louisville; South Coast Repertory, Costa Mesa). The play received numerous awards, including the American Theatre Critics Association New Play Award, Dramatists Guild/Hull-Warriner Award, Lucille Lortel Award, Outer Critics Circle Award and a Drama Desk nomination, and has been produced all over the United States and around the world.

In addition to his adaptation of *God of Vengeance*, his many plays include *Collected Stories* (Theatre Royal Haymarket, London, with Dame Helen Mirren; South Coast Repertory; Manhattan Theatre Club; HB Studio/Lucille Lortel Theatre, New York, with Uta Hagen), which received the Los Angeles Drama Critics Circle/Ted Schmitt Award, L.A. Ovation Award, a Drama Desk nomination, and was a finalist for both the Dramatists Guild/Hull-Warriner Award and the Pulitzer Prize; *Sight Unseen* (South Coast Repertory, Manhattan Theatre Club/Orpheum Theatre), which received an OBIE Award for Best New American Play, Dramatists Guild/Hull-Warriner Award, a Drama Desk nomination, and was also a Pulitzer finalist; *The Model Apartment* (Los Angeles Theatre Center; Primary Stages, New York), which received the OBIE Award for Playwriting, Drama-Logue Award, a Drama Desk nomination, and was also a Dramatists Guild/Hull-Warriner Award finalist; *The Loman Family Picnic* (Manhattan Theatre Club), which received a Drama Desk nomination; *What's Wrong with This Picture?* (Manhattan Theatre Club; Jewish Repertory Theatre, New York; on Broadway at the Brooks Atkinson Theatre); *Two Days* (Long Wharf Theatre, New Haven); *Broken Sleep: Three Plays* (Williamstown Theatre Festival); *July 7, 1994* (Actors Theatre of Louisville); *Found a Peanut* (The Joseph Papp Public Theater/New York Shakespeare Festival); *Pitching to the Star* (West Bank Cafe, New York); *Resting Place* (Theater for the New City, New York); *Gifted Children*; *Zimmer* and *Luna Park* (the last three all receiving productions at the Jewish Repertory Theatre).

*Sight Unseen* will receive its Broadway premiere in May 2004 at the Biltmore Theatre and his new play, *Brooklyn Boy*, which was commissioned by South Coast Repertory, will have its world premiere there in Fall 2004, to be followed by productions in Paris and New York.

Mr. Margulies has received grants from the National Endowment for the Arts, the New York Foundation for the Arts and the John Simon Guggenheim Memorial Foundation. He was the recipient of the 2000 Sidney Kingsley Award for Outstanding Achievement in Theatre. Mr. Margulies is an alumnus of New Dramatists and serves on the council of The Dramatists Guild of America. He holds a Bachelor of Fine Arts degree (Visual Arts, 1977) from Purchase College of the State University of New York.

Born in Brooklyn, New York, in 1954, Mr. Margulies currently lives with his wife Lynn Street, who is a physician, and their son Miles, in New Haven, Connecticut, where he teaches playwriting at Yale University.